TOGETHER

Hubert Davis led UNC to the national championship game in his first season as a college head coach.

PHOTO BY MAGGIE HOBSON

TOGETHER

THE AMAZING STORY OF
CAROLINA BASKETBALL'S
2021-2022 SEASON

ADAM LUCAS, STEVE KIRSCHNER & MATT BOWERS

FOREWORD BY HUBERT DAVIS

University of North Carolina at Chapel Hill Department of Athletics

Set in Sentinel and Gotham
by Lindsay Starr
Manufactured in the United States of America

Front cover: Head Coach Hubert Davis
Back cover: Caleb Love's three-pointer with 24 seconds
to play against Duke will go down as one of the most
memorable shots in Carolina basketball history.
Photos by Maggie Hobson

LIBRARY OF CONGRESS CATALOGING-IN-PUBLICATION DATA

Names: Lucas, Adam, 1977- author. | Kirschner, Steve (Steven A.), author. |
    Bowers, Matt, author. | Davis, Hubert, 1970- writer of foreword.
Title: Together : the amazing story of Carolina basketball's 2021-2022
    season / Adam Lucas, Steve Kirschner, and Matt Bowers.
Description: Chapel Hill : The University of North Carolina at Chapel Hill
    Department of Athletics, 2022.
Identifiers: LCCN 2022025474 | ISBN 9781469672762 (cloth ; alk. paper) |
    ISBN 9781469672779 (ebook)
Subjects: LCSH: Davis, Hubert, 1970- | University of North Carolina at
    Chapel Hill—Basketball—History—21st century. | North Carolina Tar
    Heels (Basketball team)—History—21st century. | NCAA Basketball
    Tournament (2022 : New Orleans, La.) | Basketball—North Carolina—
    Chapel Hill—History—21st century. | African American basketball
    coaches—North Carolina. | BISAC: SPORTS & RECREATION /
    Basketball | SPORTS & RECREATION / History
Classification: LCC GV884.D373 L83 2022 | DDC 796.323/6309756565—
    dc23/eng/20220627
LC record available at https://lccn.loc.gov/2022025474

CONTENTS

Hubert Davis with his family, Gracie, Elijah, Leslie, and Micah, following the Tar Heels' Elite Eight win over Saint Peter's.

PHOTO BY J. D. LYON JR.

FOREWORD

Coach Dean Smith often said, "It is amazing what you can accomplish when you don't care who gets the credit." We might not have started the season playing this way, but it is definitely how we ended it.

I was asked often throughout March Madness about how our basketball team went from clinging to the bubble to playing for the national championship. Well, I never thought we were on the bubble. It was strange to me that analysts could look at a team that was a game or two out of first place all season in the ACC and think we were not going to make the NCAA Tournament. We were 8–3 on the road, which is difficult to accomplish for any team, and we played well at home.

We had problems with consistency. We played so well against Purdue, which was the best team we faced all season, and then struggled against Tennessee the next day. We beat a solid Michigan team and then couldn't pull it together against Kentucky.

But there was no secret I can share that led to our run to the Final Four and the national championship game. There was not a game or a single practice that turned the page. The team's chemistry developed over a season when new coaches and players got a little better every day, players figured out their roles more clearly and accepted them, and everyone began listening to one another. Most important, we had talented young men who refused to give up trying.

Armando Bacot became one of the most productive players in the country; Leaky Black routinely locked down the other team's top perimeter threat and found more ways to contribute offensively; RJ Davis and Caleb Love—two young guards who improved so much in every aspect of the game—hit their strides; Brady Manek became more comfortable with his teammates and they with him, and he became the best shooting big man in the game; and our reserves began to help us win in their own unique ways.

It is no secret that we suffered some tough losses in the ACC. When we lost consecutive games at Miami and Wake Forest, I never thought those meant we were a bad team; we just had a bad week. Coach Smith taught me players need confidence more than they need criticism. My message to the team came from Proverbs 4:25: "Keep your eyes straight ahead; ignore all sideshow distractions." I told them to turn off the noise from their phones, family, friends, and fans. We needed to focus on what we could do as a basketball team and leave everyone else out of it.

Head coach Hubert Davis with Armando Bacot and Caleb Love at a press conference in New Orleans.
PHOTO BY MAGGIE HOBSON

Our coaching staff all played at North Carolina. Together, we desperately wanted the players to have their own stories. They had heard enough of ours that included ACC regular-season and Tournament championships, Sweet 16s, Final Fours, and national championships. We wanted them to know the thrill of victory in those milestones. They started to see their own stories develop after we won on the road at Virginia Tech; their confidence grew after a great win against Syracuse on Senior Night in the Smith Center; and they really began to get it after our win at Duke to end the regular season.

I spoke a lot earlier in the season about coaching effort and about playing for the name on the front of the jersey. I know I sounded like a broken record at practice and in the huddle. But they heard me. They quieted the noise and started making their own memories. And they believed in themselves the same way I believed in them.

No one thought we had a chance to win at Duke—no one. We had not played well against the Blue Devils in Chapel Hill and no one expected that to change, especially considering the celebration Duke was holding at Cameron that day. Leading up to that game, we talked very little about basketball. Instead, we talked about taking a stand, holding your ground, and being willing to fight. I was proud of the fight our players had that night. They believed if we would defend, rebound, and take care of the ball we would win. They were listening and shutting out the noise. Their gaze was fixed straight ahead on a championship, and our celebration that night is one we will never forget.

Following the win at Duke, our players understood the magnitude of what it means to play at Carolina. They were not ready for the season to end and did not care whom we were selected to play in the NCAA Tournament. They believed they could win it all. After each amazing victory—Marquette, Baylor, UCLA, Saint Peter's, and Duke—their confidence in one another grew.

The national championship game did not go our way, and that loss is tough. But this team was special. They came together when they needed to. They listened more than they gave their opinions. They stood their ground and fought as a team. I will not spend a moment being anything other than proud of these young men for an unbelievable season.

They will never forget what they accomplished this year. These are their Carolina moments forever. And they created them TOGETHER.

—Hubert Davis,
April 2022

MANEK
45

TOGE

Hubert Davis became the fourth former UNC player and first Black head coach in the program's history.

PHOTO BY JEFFREY A. CAMARATI

1

First Impressions

In his first summer as the University of North Carolina's head basketball coach, Hubert Davis had several key priorities.

He had to select a coaching staff, of course. He needed to move into the much larger head coach's office at the end of the hall in the Carolina basketball suite at the Dean Smith Center. He had to build a roster for the 2021–22 season and beyond, both through the transfer portal and through the more traditional recruitment of high school prospects.

Oh, and he had to drive the airport shuttle.

As soon as he was introduced as Carolina's head coach, Davis proclaimed, "I can't coach you if I don't know you." He already knew the returning members of the roster, having worked with them as an assistant coach. But this was different. Now he wanted to take every available opportunity to understand more about the players on his roster. So he personally drove players to and from the airport whenever he had the chance over the summer break.

As a parent of teenagers himself, Davis knew that those minutes in the car are sometimes the most insightful moments. Turn up the radio, put down the phone, and just chat about what's happening in the world and in their lives.

Davis also instituted a new rule that required players to stop by the basketball office at least three times per week. In recent years, the Tar Heels had become accustomed to entering the Smith Center through a downstairs entrance and going straight to the ground-floor players' lounge and locker room. But Davis remembered a different time, when he and other 1980s- and 1990s-era Tar Heels had spent frequent pre- and post-practice moments chatting with coaches and members of the office staff.

Davis especially treasured his relationship with office administrator Linda Woods, better known as Mama Woods to his generation of Tar Heels. He would eventually request that Woods be in the home tunnel before the game against Loyola Maryland, his first regular-season game as head coach. Just before he took the court for the first time, the pair greeted each other with a long hug that became even more meaningful when Woods passed away later in the season after a long battle with cancer.

Those are the types of bonds that have long distinguished the Carolina basketball program—the essence of what is often called the Carolina Family. While Davis was taking steps to modernize the program in other ways, he wanted to make sure some of the key priorities of the past weren't lost.

It was a throwback that initially puzzled the players.

"Sometimes I would be hardheaded and not go by there the amount of times he said we had to," admitted Caleb Love. "In looking back, though, it makes sense. You do need a relationship not only with the head coach but with everyone else on the staff. When I reflect on the season, I understand why he wanted us to do it, and I understand that it genuinely made a difference that Coach Davis made an effort to get to know us. Who doesn't want to play for a coach like that?"

"He wanted to build a bond with us," said RJ Davis. "It wasn't like he was forcing us to spend a really long time in the office. He wanted to be able to see us on the basketball court but also away from the basketball court. That's

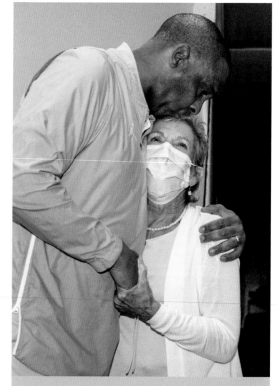

Linda Woods was Dean Smith's and Bill Guthridge's executive assistant and was an important fixture in the program for more than 30 years.
PHOTO BY MAGGIE HOBSON

Caleb Love represented the Tar Heels on ACC Media Day in Charlotte.
PHOTO BY MAGGIE HOBSON

what built that chemistry between all of us that eventually translated to the court. That's why this team was so tight. We loved being around each other, and it showed."

Hubert Davis also reached out to the players in a meaningful way. Roy Williams had been fond of saying he was "not of their generation," which meant he didn't always appreciate the major way that seemingly minor details such as headbands, alternate jerseys, or specific kinds of shoes might matter to his players. In fact, one of the most legendary outbursts of the Williams era came after a small group of Tar Heels wore headbands during a listless November 2006 loss to Gonzaga. The head coach quickly informed his players the headbands would never be seen again—and they weren't.

But Davis, who wasn't that far removed from his 12-year NBA playing career, understood how meaningful such details could be. So in the first team meeting with him as head coach, he asked his players a very simple question: "What's important to you?"

The answer led to the Tar Heels wearing black uniforms in a game—the disappointing loss to Kentucky in the CBS Sports Classic in Las Vegas—for the first time since 2015. The policy forbidding players from wearing retro Air Jordan sneakers during game action was relaxed, which especially pleased noted sneakerhead Caleb Love.

"When Coach Davis asked us how we wanted things to be different, that really meant a lot to us," said Armando Bacot. "He didn't promise to do everything we asked for, but he heard us on a lot of those requests. Being able to do things like wear sleeves or headbands or different-colored shoes mattered to us. We all grew up playing AAU basketball and being able to do our own thing. Fashion has become a big part of basketball. It's a new-age type of thing, and he adjusted to that because we said it was important."

Tar Heel players and coaches wore sweatshirts promoting social causes to the game at NC State. PHOTO BY MAGGIE HOBSON

Team rules restricting the wearing of retro Air Jordans were relaxed.
PHOTO BY MAGGIE HOBSON

Hubert Davis's allowance to the players to wear uniform accessories was well received by the players. PHOTO BY MAGGIE HOBSON

Against Kentucky the Tar Heels broke out black uniforms for the first time in six seasons.
PHOTO BY MAGGIE HOBSON

Carolina players cheered on their fellow Tar Heels at a football game.
PHOTO BY MAGGIE HOBSON

The outside perception that Davis was simply going to clone Roy Williams's program quickly proved to be inaccurate. It's true that Davis built his staff with a desire to replicate some of the same experiences he'd enjoyed as a Tar Heel player, and he kept existing coaching staff members Sean May and Brad Frederick to maintain some continuity. But he also made an immediate phone call to Jeff Lebo. The renowned Tar Heel point guard and longtime college coach had returned to the high school ranks as an assistant coach for West Carteret High School, and he and his wife, Melissa (also a Carolina graduate), were on the verge of building their dream post-coaching home near the water.

Davis called while Lebo was power washing his deck one afternoon. Lebo had been a veteran leader at UNC when Davis was a player and was instrumental in absorbing Davis into the Carolina basketball program. Davis maintained significant respect for his mentor over the next several decades and knew he wanted Lebo to be part of his staff.

Melissa Lebo, though, wasn't initially thrilled about the prospect of returning to the coaching life.

"I need to talk to you about a coaching opportunity," Jeff told her when he came inside.

"Oh no," she said.

"It's at Carolina," her husband replied.

Melissa didn't even pause before saying, "When do we leave?"

That's the type of love for the university and the basketball program that Davis wanted to permeate his staff. He added Brandon Robinson as a graduate manager, a player to whom Davis had become very close during Robinson's playing career. He hired Pat Sullivan, who had worked as a Carolina assistant from 1997 to 2000 and who had made multiple coaching stops in the NBA. At each one of those stops, he made clear his love for the Tar Heels—so much so that when he informed the head coach of his current employer, the Minnesota Timberwolves, of his job opportunity in Chapel Hill, Chris Finch immediately replied, "You right?"

Sophomores Puff Johnson and RJ Davis on the first day of fall classes.
PHOTO BY MAGGIE HOBSON

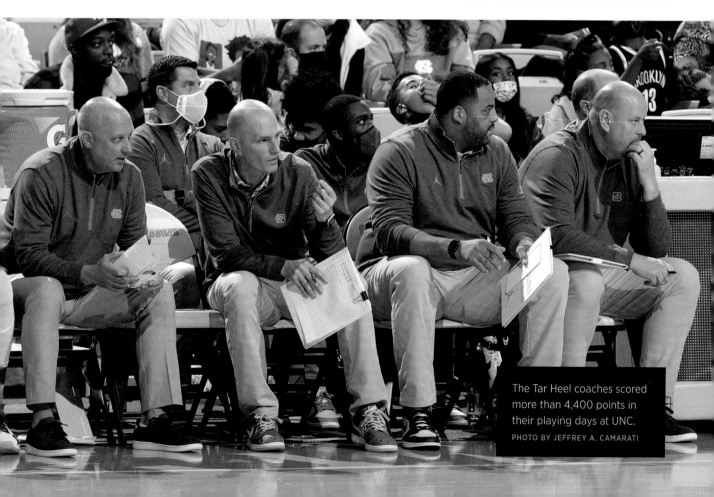

The Tar Heel coaches scored more than 4,400 points in their playing days at UNC.
PHOTO BY JEFFREY A. CAMARATI

Carolina kicked off the new season with a Blue-White scrimmage on October 15, 2021.

Sullivan was hired to strengthen the program in the area of skill development, a constant emphasis from Davis in his early weeks as head coach. He wanted Tar Heel players to be able to work out anytime and wanted them to have the resources not just to fire up a few jump shots in the Smith Center but go through an intense, pro-style routine. Visiting pros and former players stopping by Chapel Hill over the summer commented about the intensity of the staff-led individual workouts.

At the same time Davis announced his bench coaching staff, he also made official the underrated hiring of Jackie Manuel. A 2005 national champion, Manuel had just completed a season on staff with the Carolina women's team. Head coach Courtney Banghart foreshadowed Manuel's impact on the 2022 men's Tar Heels when she said, "Jackie meets people where they need to be met. His humility is his superpower, and his care for others is his biggest asset. He is a positive energy force always. He communicates honestly and is others-oriented to the core. He listens, he observes, and he cares."

In the midst of the new hiring, there was surprisingly little in-depth investigation of what kind of coach Davis actually wanted to be. Roy Williams had a distinctly Carolina background—his entire college coaching experience had been under Dean Smith until he took over his own program at Kansas in 1988.

But Davis was different. He'd played in the NBA under a variety of head coaches, including legends Don Nelson and Pat Riley. He was always a Tar Heel, of course. But his years in the pro game had a swift impact. His constant emphasis on skill development came from Nelson.

Davis also made adjustments to the way Carolina prepared for opponents, using an in-depth scouting process that he learned partially from Riley. He prepared specific plays he believed would work against each individual opponent, identifying weak points and preparing his team to attack them repeatedly.

Hubert Davis's Tar Heels were picked to finish fourth in the ACC by the media in the preseason poll.
PHOTO BY MAGGIE HOBSON

Raleigh native Justin McKoy came to UNC after playing two seasons at ACC rival Virginia.

Davis also had spent seven seasons with ESPN, where his role with *College GameDay* allowed him to observe practices and have informal conversations with the nation's best college coaches. "From being with ESPN, I can't tell you how many practices and shootarounds and games from other schools I attended," Davis said. "So many times, I would see something and say, 'I like that' or 'I didn't know you could do it this way.' It was awesome. Because even though it confirmed my belief in the way that we played at Carolina, it also enabled me to see some of the same things a little differently and showed me other ways to do things.

"For example," Davis continued, "I got a couple of our zone offense plays from Rick Pitino. One of our defensive tweaks comes from Tom Izzo. I learned from Mike Krzyzewski that plays don't have to be complicated. He showed me you can run simple plays that put the opponent in a pinch, and if we run a play and it works, we're going back to it again until you stop it. That's not typically the way Carolina has done it."

Graduate student Brady Manek transferred to UNC after four seasons at Oklahoma, where he was OU's 14th-leading scorer of all-time.
PHOTO BY MAGGIE HOBSON

Davis was also immediately up front with his players about their professional aspirations. The NBA was likely mentioned more at a handful of summer workouts than it had been the entire 2020–21 season. Davis believed in acknowledging the dreams of his players—but also in making it very clear how he and the Tar Heel coaching staff could help them realize those dreams.

The outside perception of Hubert Davis continued to be of a happy, never-negative head coach. Tar Heel players quickly learned their new coach had no problem being tough when the situation called for it. In one summer workout, Davis paused the action and looked at Armando Bacot. "Armando," he told him, "when you're in the NBA and you mess up, you're not going to get a hug like what I give you. You're going to get cut."

"My first two years, Coach Davis was nowhere near as vocal," Bacot said. "But he set the tone as a head coach at our first summer practice. We were doing the shell drill. With me coming back, I thought I was going to be the star player and people would probably go easy on me. He went at me in that very first practice. It was tough. I was so surprised, because I had never seen him yell like that. For him to come at me in front of everyone on the very first day set the tone early and got our respect right away." •

The Tar Heels returned four starters from the 2020–21 team that lost in the first round of the NCAA Tournament.

PHOTO BY MAGGIE HOBSON

Brady Manek hit four threes and scored a team-high 24 points in the win at Louisville.

PHOTO BY MAGGIE HOBSON

New Faces

One of Hubert Davis's best moves in his first month as North Carolina's head coach was a Google search.

Faced with a depleted roster that wasn't necessarily suited to playing Davis's preferred style, he went to his Smith Center office in his first few days on the job and typed in a very simple search: "2021 college basketball best transfer portal players."

The resulting research led him to an Oklahoma standout named Brady Manek. The fit seemed promising. On first glance, at six foot nine, Manek looked like a post player. But a deeper look at his profile revealed a three-point marksman who had been a four-year contributor for the Sooners while earning third-team Academic All-America honors. After two minutes watching Manek's highlights on the Synergy video system, Davis was intrigued.

On a Monday in April, he called Manek but was unable to reach him. On Tuesday, the pair connected for a Zoom call. Before that call, Manek and his very close-knit family had narrowed it down to three choices: return to Oklahoma, turn professional, or transfer to Carolina.

UNC · 83
Loyola Maryland · 67
NOVEMBER 9, 2021

UNC · 94
Brown · 87
NOVEMBER 12, 2021

The Hubert Davis era at Carolina officially began with an 83–67 win in the Smith Center over Loyola Maryland in Davis's first game as head coach.

Brady Manek hit Carolina's first basket of the season and his first as a Tar Heel, a three-pointer from the right wing, just 17 seconds into the contest.

Caleb Love quickly flashed improved play from his erratic freshman season, scoring a game-high 22 points on seven of 13 shooting without committing a turnover. Kerwin Walton scored a season-high 11 points, hitting a trio

of three-pointers as UNC improved to 100–12 in season openers and won its 20th consecutive home opener.

Three days later, Brown University came into the Smith Center and gave the Tar Heels a scare, blistering the nets and leading for most of the game. The Bears scored 50 first-half points on 1.28 points per possession and led by as many as six points several times, including with just over 12 minutes to play.

Carolina didn't take its first second-half lead until 9:44 remained to play, and it didn't lead for good until two minutes

later. Over the final eight minutes of the game, UNC's defense limited Brown to just five of 18 shooting from the floor (after the Bears had shot 58.2 percent up to that point).

RJ Davis set career highs with 26 points and six three-pointers, including four in the final 6:55 of action. Armando Bacot posted his first double-double of the season with 22 points and 10 rebounds, hitting 10 of 11 shots.

By the end of the call, the Manek family decided the two best choices were either turning pro or becoming a Tar Heel. And by Friday, the Harrah, Oklahoma, native who had played his entire college career less than an hour from his hometown had committed to a college he had never seen in person that was located halfway across the country.

"When I think about it now, I'm even more surprised that I did it," Manek said a year later. "I'm not the kind of person to just pack up and leave and move across the country."

Plenty of other schools had called Manek to gauge his interest in transferring. But none of them connected the same way Davis did. "We made the decision together as a family," Manek said. "Because of the history at Carolina and the opportunity to have that Carolina experience for one year, we decided it was something I couldn't pass up."

Making the decision meant Manek packed up his beloved white muscle car with lime green racing stripes (Manek named the car "Larry") and drove 1,178 miles to his new home.

RJ Davis made six three-pointers and set an early career scoring high with 26 points in a hard-fought win over Brown.
PHOTO BY MAGGIE HOBSON

That made Manek the newest member of a rapidly reshaping roster. Davis proved himself nimble at a time when many coaches at blue-chip programs still seemed unsure how to adjust to the transfer portal's effect on the college game. Davis's first addition was Virginia transfer Justin McKoy, a versatile forward who could shoot out to the three-point line but also defend in the post. Freshmen Dontrez Styles and D'Marco Dunn were Roy Williams signees who arrived in the summer for orientation. Marquette transfer Dawson Garcia officially announced his intention to become a Tar Heel in early July. The additions dramatically overhauled a roster that had lost Garrison Brooks, who transferred to play a fifth year at Mississippi State; Walker Kessler, who moved to Auburn; fellow big men Walker Miller and Sterling Manley, who also decided to play the 2021–22 season elsewhere; and Day'Ron Sharpe, who went to the NBA. Without the new additions, departures would have left Armando Bacot as the only true returning post presence on the team.

Freshman guard D'Marco Dunn was one of seven newcomers on the 2021–22 Tar Heel roster.
PHOTO BY ANTHONY SORBELLINI

UNC · 94
College of Charleston · 83

Armando Bacot dominated the paint at Charleston with 24 points, 12 boards, and six blocks.

PHOTO BY MAGGIE HOBSON

It was a mostly under-the-radar non-conference game in November, but Carolina's 94–83 win at Charleston foretold several of the major story lines that would play out over the next five months.

Hubert Davis took his team on the road for the first time as head coach, and the capacity crowd proved to be one of the most hostile environments the Tar Heels would play in all season.

The Cougars came out firing, making five of their first seven field goals from three-point range, and built a 26–15 lead. Armando Bacot scored 16 of his then career-high 24 points in the first half to close the gap to six at the break.

The second half saw a number of trends emerge that would seemingly follow UNC all season: Bacot continued to dominate inside, finishing with a dozen boards and six blocks; Caleb Love calmly sank 10 of 12 from the free throw line and scored 18 second-half points; Brady Manek made a pair of threes in a 12–4 run to start the half; Leaky Black held Charleston's leading scorer, John Meeks, to two of 14 field goals and seven points, half his season average; and the Tar Heels shot 64.3 percent from the floor over the final 20 minutes, during which they outscored the Cougars, 58–41.

Bacot made 10 of 12 field goals, which, combined with his performance against Brown, made him the first Tar Heel ever with 20 points, 10 rebounds, and 80 percent shooting from the floor in consecutive games.

The Tar Heels would go on to an 8–3 road record, well above the national average that saw visiting teams win less than 43 percent of their games.

Purdue · 93
UNC · 84

Carolina brought its 3–0 record and no. 18 Associated Press ranking to the Mohegan Sun Casino in Connecticut the week before Thanksgiving to play in the Basketball Hall of Fame Tip-Off Tournament.

The Tar Heels would depart the Nutmeg State with their first two-game losing streak in the Hubert Davis era and a departure from the national rankings until early March.

Purdue looked the part of a national championship contender in its 93–84 win over the Tar Heels, although Carolina, playing without Leaky Black, who was sick, battled hard all game and took a brief lead in the second half.

National Player of the Year candidate Jaden Ivey was one of three Boilermakers to score 20 or more points. The lightning-quick guard had 22 points, 10 rebounds, and six assists; Sasha Stefanovic made five threes and scored 23 points; and beefy forward Trevion Williams scored 18 of his 20 in the second half.

Dawson Garcia made all seven of his field goal attempts in the first half as he scored 15 of his season-high 26 points to keep the Tar Heels within striking distance. Garcia's three with 9:19 to play in the game gave Carolina a 65–64 lead, its only lead of the game, but Purdue answered with a 10–0 run over the next 90 seconds to secure the outcome.

Garcia, RJ Davis (with 18 points), and Caleb Love (18) combined for 62 of UNC's 84 points, while Armando Bacot, battling Williams and seven-foot-four center Zach Edey, went one for six with a season-low two points.

Tennessee · 89
UNC · 72

Purdue's second-half shooting, explosive scoring, and ability to convert Tar Heel turnovers into points proved to be a precursor of things to come the following day against Tennessee and in losses throughout the season.

The Tennessee game went south early as UNC struggled to keep the ball from getting inside by dribble or pass as the Volunteers scored 54 paint points and had 28 assists on 38 baskets in a 17-point win. Tennessee led by seven at the break and opened the second half on a 7–2 run, eventually stretching its lead to 20.

Brady Manek hit a season-high six threes and scored 24 points, but UNC was outscored, 19–8, on the break and gave up 19 points off turnovers for the second consecutive game.

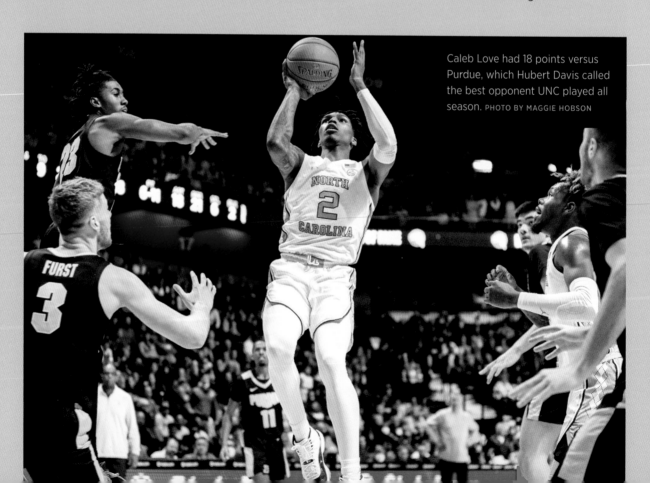

Caleb Love had 18 points versus Purdue, which Hubert Davis called the best opponent UNC played all season. PHOTO BY MAGGIE HOBSON

Dawson Garcia scored
a season-best 26 points
against Purdue.

PHOTO BY MAGGIE HOBSON

Manek's addition left his future Tar Heel teammates especially curious.

"I had no idea who Brady Manek was at all," Bacot said. "We all had this idea of him as being from Oklahoma and being some country guy, wearing cowboy boots and Wrangler jeans."

"My first thought was 'That guy is my roommate?'" said Leaky Black of his first meeting with Manek and his long red beard and flowing locks. "I knew he had never set foot in North Carolina but he committed to us, so I took it upon myself to make sure he had a good experience here."

Black, a Concord native who was perhaps the most introverted player on the roster, was at first an unlikely fit for Manek, a fiery presence who was rarely spotted without his Bass Pro Shops hat. His eclectic style had won him some attention as a Sooner ("My first reaction was 'We have Larry Bird on the team now,'" said RJ Davis), but looking beyond the hair and the beard revealed a savvy, well-rounded player.

Manek won teammates over immediately in summer pickup with his blend of court awareness and accurate shooting. His reputation had been well earned as a perimeter sniper, and he demonstrated that same touch on a regular basis. But his knowledge of the game had not been as widely advertised, and teammates soon learned he was equally capable of finding them with a well-timed pass.

And he did it all with a slightly unexpected swagger. "As soon as he got here, he was talking junk," Bacot said. "He had an edge that you might not have expected. You think of him as this spot-up shooter who isn't mixing it up, but if you throw a punch at him, he's going to punch back."

Manek's competitiveness was tested by Carolina's early rotation. He started in the season opener against Loyola Maryland and performed very well, scoring 20 points in 29 minutes. But he came off the bench in the next dozen games, as Davis instead used Garcia in the starting lineup.

The first-year head coach recognized very early in practice that he was facing a difficult decision. Both Garcia and Manek were productive players. Both were going to contribute to a successful Tar Heel team.

But Davis remembered a discussion he'd had with Roy Williams regarding the 2005 national championship team's rotation. Marvin Williams came off the bench that entire season, although he was an extremely

Brady Manek scored 24 points versus Tennessee, one of 10 games in which he scored at least 20 points.
PHOTO BY MAGGIE HOBSON

Dawson Garcia scored more than 20 points in back-to-back games against Elon and Furman.

productive player. That allowed Jawad Williams to remain in the starting lineup. Either would have been a defensible starting choice. But Roy Williams told Davis he kept Marvin in a reserve role because he felt the freshman was better prepared to handle that job than the senior, just as Jawad's veteran ACC experience made him a good fit to begin games. It had very little to do with points, rebounds, or assists and was much more dependent on the right blend of production and team chemistry.

"At the beginning of the year, I talked to Armando, Dawson, and Brady, because all three of them are starter-type players," Davis said. "I even wanted to look at playing all three of them together and playing big, because I felt like we could do it."

That type of lineup probably would have worked at the NBA level. In college, though, the Tar Heels needed more flexibility. And using the wisdom he'd received from Roy Williams regarding the 2005 team, Davis decided Manek's demeanor was better equipped to handle not starting.

Manek never outwardly complained. But that didn't mean his competitive nature wasn't challenged by the arrangement. This was a player who had spent most of his basketball career feeling undervalued. He didn't

Brady Manek led UNC with 22 points in an overtime win in his final game in the Smith Center and was named ACC Player of the Week for his efforts.

receive the hype of many flashier players and had never been the headliner despite consistently outperforming many better-known players. So the situation required the first-year head coach to demonstrate a steady hand to ensure Manek knew that the team understood his value.

"Coach Davis talked to me about it and said he knew I'd be able to handle it," Manek said. "He knew I was reliable but said we needed to try and preserve other pieces of the team. But I definitely was thinking about it. I knew what kind of numbers I was putting up. I wanted to make sure I was helping the team when I came off the bench. And the way things worked out, by the end of the season, it felt like I had been starting the whole year."

Garcia was injured in the opening minutes of Carolina's win at Boston College on January 2 and struggled to get comfortable after the injury, making just three of his final 26 shot attempts as a Tar Heel and shooting just four for 18 when he came off the bench for three games after his return—well below his previous season-long shooting percentage that hovered near 45 percent.

The Minnesota native eventually made the difficult decision to return home to help deal with lingering health issues affecting multiple members of his family. Manek's role increased immediately, and he shot better than 50 percent over the remainder of the season.

Leaky Black didn't play versus Purdue due to illness but returned to the lineup the next day in the loss to Tennessee.

PHOTO BY MAGGIE HOBSON

He earned All–East Region honors in the NCAA Tournament and tied for Carolina's leading scorer during the six NCAA Tournament games. He also became a Chapel Hill folk hero, as the same characteristics that endeared him to his teammates also proved to be irresistible to fans.

It's true Manek was a unique representative of a program in which Dean Smith once required James Worthy to provide medical proof of a skin condition in order to sport one of the only beards in the Smith era. But it's also true that fans gravitated to the passion Manek demonstrated daily on the court in addition to his uncanny ability to get off his reliable three-point jumper with only a sliver of daylight available.

Manek's parents became fixtures in the Smith Center and arenas throughout the ACC. By the time he finished his Tar Heel career, he had played only four college games without at least one parent present. That was an especially remarkable statistic given that his older brother, Kellen, was also a college basketball player, for Southeastern Oklahoma State. That led to some unusual Manek family itineraries; it wasn't unusual for Tina and Cary Manek to see four games in four different states in four days.

Tina had left Chapel Hill in tears after moving her son in over the summer. But her phone conversations with him in the following days reassured her that he was comfortable and in the right place.

And as his minutes increased throughout January and February, so did his comfort level with his teammates on and off the court. Near the end of January, in a conversation in the head coach's office, Davis told Manek his teammates wanted to hear even more from him. "This is your first year here, but you've been through the Big 12," Davis told him. "The guys will listen to you because of your knowledge and experience. Your teammates love you, and they want to hear from you."

As he got to know him better, Davis observed that Manek was his own worst critic, sometimes getting so frustrated with one missed shot that it took him out of the rhythm of the game. But the head coach loved his passion and the fact that all of Manek's emotion was directed toward only one goal: winning.

Even when a raucous late-game atmosphere in a February 1 win at Louisville prompted some heated words from Manek in a Tar Heel huddle, Davis didn't mind. The object of Manek's outburst was very simple: he wanted to help Carolina find a way to win. And the Tar Heels did, surviving in overtime with Manek contributing 24 points and playing all but four minutes of the game. Amid a ferocious atmosphere that included fans throwing debris onto the court, it was the type of tough road victory the Tar Heels needed to demonstrate they were making progress, even though much of the nation wasn't noticing.

It was also the perfect testament to the production and grit Manek brought to the team. Reflecting on the evolving relationship he experienced with his new roommate over the course of the year, Black summarized it perfectly. "I've never been around someone like him before," the senior said. "He's so genuine and he's so easy to be around. He makes it look so easy. He's a hothead, but we're so opposite that it attracted. I think he might be my favorite player." •

Brady Manek chose Carolina to advance beyond the second round of the NCAA Tournament; he did that and also earned All-East Regional honors and posted a double-double versus Kansas in the national championship game.

PHOTO BY MAGGIE HOBSON

Carolina struggled to find consistent play in the early part of the season, falling out of the polls after a pair of losses in Connecticut in November.

PHOTO BY MAGGIE HOBSON

3

Absent of My Personality

Hubert Davis spent nine years as an assistant coach at UNC before being named the head coach in April 2021.

PHOTO BY MAGGIE HOBSON

By the time the Tar Heels made it to New Orleans, a generally accepted national portrait of Hubert Davis had begun to emerge. That image—of a relentlessly positive optimist who guided his team with a pat on the back and steady encouragement—was partially true.

The full picture, though, is much more complex. This is, after all, a head coach who spent several years on national television, who is described by almost everyone who knows him as one of the kindest people they know, and yet who candidly says, "I am not a people person."

That might be a confusing self-description to those who know only the television version of Davis. But one of the most difficult aspects of his first year as Carolina's head coach was finding a way to balance the constant need to be the public face of the program—within days of getting the job, he was asked for dozens of pictures at one of his children's lacrosse games, a phenomenon that had never occurred when he was an assistant—with what he knew about himself.

"I'm not a quiet person, but I don't like noise," he said. "I need time by myself. I enjoy being by myself and being with my family. I don't like distractions. When I'm at practice, I am fully at practice. I don't sit around and talk to people who come to practice. At shootaround, I am fully at shootaround. I'm locked into what my job is. Sometimes people might misinterpret that as being quiet.

"It's true that I don't seek out being around people. My wife, Leslie, does that. She passionately enjoys being around people and having conversations. That's not me. I don't dislike people. But I need that time when I'm by myself."

Combine the new job with the fact that Davis—a fully committed father who is deeply involved with his three children—was navigating the responsibilities of the new job in the same fall that his oldest child left for college out of state, and it was an emotional few months. Anyone whose oldest child has ever left for college knows that the dynamic at home changes. "It was hard," Davis said. "Everyone kept saying it's a great thing when your child leaves. It wasn't. It stinks. A personality that has been in the house for 18 years is gone. That was very difficult to handle."

Numerous Tar Heels said Hubert Davis's reaction to a pair of blowout losses at Miami and Wake Forest was key to the team's midseason resurgence.
PHOTO BY MAGGIE HOBSON

One of the biggest misconceptions of Hubert Davis was that he is soft-spoken and reserved. "I'm not quiet," says Davis.

Davis was also concerned about the impact his new job would have on his wife and his two children who were still in public school in the area. Now, he knew, Dad's job would be the topic of almost daily conversation with their friends. Carolina losing a basketball game wouldn't impact just his daily life. It was going to change theirs, too.

Perhaps the relatable stress the head coach was facing made it even more remarkable that Davis made it through his entire first year as North Carolina's head coach without cursing once. Of course, he blistered his team on multiple occasions. It's just that he managed to do it with an entirely different vocabulary, one that immediately required his players to understand his use of the multipurpose word "bejeebies" (as in "What the bejeebies is that?" or as an exclamatory "Bejeebies!" when perusing a particularly noteworthy box score).

The Tar Heels also had to adjust to perhaps Davis's most heated, most intense comment: "Fart that crap!" Used as a substitute for a more vulgar exclamation, Davis used the phrase both during practice when frustrated with his team's effort and in a couple different pregame speeches. It frequently caught his players, all of whom had been brought up in a more unrefined basketball environment, by surprise.

"Coach Davis is such a powerful motivational speaker," said Leaky Black. "He'll get going before games, and he's got you almost about to cry because you are so ready to play. And then he'll throw out a 'bejeebies' or a 'fart that crap' and you're not expecting it. You still get the message. But it takes some adjustment."

And that is how some observers underestimate Davis. They wrongly believe that his refusal to use coarse language somehow indicates a softness or an unwillingness to compete.

A reminder: as a player, Hubert Davis was a member of the mid-1990s New York Knicks teams that included John Starks, Anthony Mason, and Charles Oakley.

"That team and our identity was very much about physical toughness," said Greg Anthony, who was Davis's teammate for three seasons on the Knicks. "In those days we didn't have the internet, so we just assumed that if the Knicks drafted a guy, he would fit in. And Hubert did. A team is like a family, and there are some who aren't exactly like the others, but you always have their back. I don't know that Hubert has ever hated anything in his life. But when it comes to competing, you won't find anyone more competitive."

Hubert Davis became the second individual to both play for and be the head coach at a school that went to the Final Four.
PHOTO BY MAGGIE HOBSON

UNC · 72
Michigan · 51

DECEMBER 1, 2021

Ten days after back-to-back losses to ranked foes Purdue and Tennessee, the Tar Heels played their best game of the nonconference season when they dominated 24th-ranked Michigan, 72–51, in the ACC/Big Ten Challenge in the Smith Center.

"I felt like our guys wanted another opportunity against a big-time team," Hubert Davis said afterward.

Michigan's 51 points were UNC's fewest allowed in its 23-game history in the Challenge, and the 21-point win was Carolina's biggest in the event since 2008.

After leading just 29–27 at halftime, the Tar Heels shot a blistering 58.1 percent in the second half, blowing open the game and outscoring the Wolverines, 43–24, in the final 20 minutes. Michigan shot just 33 percent from the floor in the second half and 35 percent overall in the game.

Caleb Love led all scorers with 22 points, his third 22-point game of the young season, hitting four three-pointers. Armando Bacot posted 11 points and a then season-high 14 rebounds, a figure that eventually would seem practically puny compared to some of his later outputs. Bacot outplayed Wolverine big man Hunter Dickinson, limiting him to just four points and five rebounds.

The win was the second of what would become a five-game winning streak. The Tar Heels held their opponents to 63 or fewer points in all five victories.

UNC · 79
Georgia Tech · 62

DECEMBER 5, 2021

Carolina went on a 22–4 run to pull away from the Yellow Jackets in the early December win in Atlanta.

PHOTO BY MAGGIE HOBSON

The Tar Heels headed to Atlanta to open ACC play at Georgia Tech. Fresh in people's minds was the previous season's 72–67 loss in Atlanta in which the Yellow Jackets overcame an eight-point Tar Heel lead over the final seven minutes.

UNC jumped out to a 12–4 advantage but Tech erupted for five straight three-pointers as part of a 19–2 run, pulling ahead by nine. However, the Tar Heels drew even at the half and went on a 12–0 run of their own early in the second to build a double-digit lead. RJ Davis and Brady Manek both scored 13 second-half points, with each connecting on a trio of three-pointers as Carolina pulled away for a 17-point victory.

Carolina shot 65.5 percent from the floor in the second half and a season-best 56.4 percent for the game. Davis scored a game-high 23 points, Armando Bacot had 13 rebounds, and Caleb Love and Davis combined for 40 points, 10 assists, and four steals.

It was Carolina's fifth win in seven games at McCamish Pavilion.

Carolina's win at Georgia Tech made UNC just the third program in NCAA history with 2,300 wins.

PHOTO BY MAGGIE HOBSON

For over 25 years, Davis forced himself every summer to watch the game film of Carolina's loss to Kansas in the 1991 Final Four. It didn't matter that he had been tremendous in that game, scoring 25 points. It only mattered that he felt he hadn't done enough to help the Tar Heels win.

Very few of the Tar Heels had seen that side of him as an assistant coach, when Roy Williams usually handled any of the barking that needed to be done. In the opening days of practice, though, they quickly learned that the head coach version of Hubert Davis had plenty of passion. In one instance, he was overseeing a new drill he'd installed called "trenches," which was basically a one-on-one battle between two Tar Heels in which they were confined to the limited space of only the painted area of the lane.

In Davis's estimation, his players were not disappointed enough when they allowed a teammate to score. The head coach stopped the drill. "It is not OK," he yelled while stalking across the lane. "Nobody should be smiling. If someone scores like that on me, something is going to happen. It is not OK to let them score. I want it to be a long night when you come to play against Carolina."

The explosion was notable enough that players were still discussing it the next day in the locker room.

"Him getting on us the way he did felt way worse than using a bunch of bad words," Armando Bacot said. "He had us all shook. That's the day we learned not to get on his bad side. It was almost like we had disappointed him, and that felt terrible. He has a way of doing it that lets you know you messed up but also encouraging you at the same time."

Davis was open to giving the players privileges, such as stylish alternate jerseys or more freedom in their game accessories. But he also demanded they return the consideration with effort. When Carolina lost two November games at Connecticut's Mohegan Sun, falling to a stout Purdue squad but then slumbering through a loss to Tennessee, Davis changed the practice schedule. The Tar Heels had previously had Thanksgiving off; now they were going to practice on the holiday.

His willingness to make a somewhat unpopular decision proved essential in the opening months of the Davis era to set the tone. But even some out-of-state players' parents understood why they were practicing rather than eating turkey at home. "My mom told me I didn't need to be coming home, because we had to get better," Bacot said.

Davis's Thought for the Day at the top of one of those Thanksgiving week practice plans perfectly summarized his message to his team: "I will never again coach a team absent of my personality."

"I knew exactly what he meant," RJ Davis said. "I'm the same way. I don't like losing, and I knew he wanted us to play with passion and toughness and energy. Looking back on it, that was the start of us regrouping and getting a better understanding of what he expected of us."

In many ways, those strict November and December practices established the foundation for a change of approach in January. With Carolina coming off routs on the road at Miami and Wake Forest, two key moments happened. First, the players met in the Smith Center locker room as soon as the bus returned from Winston-Salem. Multiple players addressed their teammates, including Duwe Farris—a walk-on with a deep family history at Carolina—who bluntly told his more highly recruited teammates they needed to figure out what was wrong.

"We can feel sorry for ourselves or we can come together," Bacot said. "We have to do this for ourselves. Stop worrying about what the media is saying and what everyone else is saying about us. We have to decide that we're better than this."

Brady Manek mostly sat quietly until near the end of the meeting. "I was still coming off the bench, so I didn't want to stand up and make a big deal," he said. "So I let everyone talk and when they asked me what I thought, I told them we had some of the best talent I've ever played with. But I've been on teams that have lost multiple games like this—and even on those teams, we didn't lose by 20 in back-to-back games. So how can we have such good talent and get blown out multiple times? That didn't make sense to me. I told them that to be successful, at some point we have to decide we want to play well for ourselves. We're not doing it because the coaches tell us to but because we take pride in playing well and we want to experience winning. I knew we were better than what we had showed."

RJ Davis said Coach Davis pushes the players to get the fire out of them, something he loves about him.
PHOTO BY MAGGIE HOBSON

Kentucky · 98
UNC · 69

DECEMBER 18, 2021

The Tar Heels entered their CBS Sports Classic matchup with the University of Kentucky riding a five-game winning streak but flew home from Las Vegas with a 29-point loss to the Wildcats, 98–69. It was UNC's biggest margin of defeat since a 33-point loss at Florida State in 2012.

Carolina originally was scheduled to play UCLA while UK was to play Ohio State in the event, but UNC played the Wildcats for the second year in a row due to COVID-related protocols in the UCLA and Ohio State programs.

The result was Kentucky's biggest win over the Tar Heels since before the formation of the ACC (an 83–44 UK win in Lexington on January 9, 1950). The Wildcats' 98 points were the most by a UNC opponent in a regulation game since Kentucky beat Carolina 103–100 five years earlier in the CBS Sports Challenge in the same arena in Las Vegas.

Carolina had its worst three-point-shooting game of the season, hitting just one of 13 as a team.

UK dominated the Tar Heels on the boards, posting a 44–26 rebounding edge that was the worst rebound margin of the season for Carolina.

Armando Bacot was one of UNC's few bright spots, tallying 22 points and 10 rebounds for his seventh double-double of the season. He scored 17 of Carolina's 29 second-half points. RJ Davis (10) was the only other Tar Heel to score in double figures.

Nothing went right for the Tar Heels in a 29-point loss to Kentucky in Las Vegas.

PHOTO BY MAGGIE HOBSON

Caleb Love's buy-in of his need to improve from his freshman season was cited early by Hubert Davis as a key to Carolina's improvement as a team. PHOTO BY MAGGIE HOBSON

A few hours later, Davis gathered his team on Sunday for a scheduled film session and practice. But first, he reviewed the list of team goals the squad had established before the season. The sheet of paper had been laminated and signed by every player. The six tangible on-court goals were as follows:

1. Win national championship.

2. Win ACC regular season/ACC Tournament.

3. Undefeated but in an event of a loss, never lose two games in a row or a home game or a rivalry game.

4. Top in the nation in offensive rebounding.

5. Have the most efficient offense and top defense in the ACC.

6. Win Mohegan Sun.

"We can still achieve the most important goals on this list," Davis told his team. "And if that's the case, why are we in such a bad mood?"

That weekend marked the beginning of the season's turnaround. Dawson Garcia left and Anthony Harris became unavailable for the rest of the season. Garcia's absence moved Manek into the starting lineup, and the lack of reserve depth meant the five starters gained some chemistry by necessity. There were no more trial combinations on the court. RJ Davis, Caleb Love, Manek, Black, and Bacot were the starting five and the primary five, with occasional meaningful contributions from Puff Johnson, Dontrez Styles, Justin McKoy, Kerwin Walton, and D'Marco Dunn. The lack of bench depth was a concern for Hubert Davis, but it was also a luxury that solved an early-season issue, because the gap between the starters and the reserves was wide enough that there wasn't much true frustration over playing time. It was obvious by the results that the right five were on the court.

The shift wasn't immediate. The win at Louisville was a solid victory, but it was followed by an 87–67 loss to Duke at the Smith Center in which the Blue Devils played one of their best games of the season and Carolina looked outclassed. Three days later, though, the Tar Heels emerged from Clemson with another gritty win. But after a rout over Florida State, Carolina inexplicably lost a home game to Pitt, a team that wouldn't win another game the rest of the season.

That loss, however, also provided one of the key moments of the season for the Tar Heel mindset. An underlying story line for much of the season had been the perception that Carolina was a soft team. One national writer described the Tar Heels that way on video in December; Davis showed his team the entire segment before they took the court against Appalachian State on December 21.

It was one thing to hear such criticism from an outsider. But after Pitt's 76–67 win at the Smith Center, a Pitt representative stood on the court and loudly boasted to his Panther players that he'd told them Carolina was soft, that he knew the Tar Heels didn't want to fight.

Several Tar Heel players took notice. It was hard not to, since the visitor was shouting in the middle of their home court.

That's when Hubert Davis began telling his team he was looking for fighters, that it was imperative for Carolina to be the team to land the first punch. He didn't want them to play dirty. But he was tired of the "soft" label being applied to Carolina, tired of an opponent disrespecting them on their home court. In many ways, Davis is still a player at heart. When he walks into the arena before the game listening to music, he usually has rapper Lil Durk queued up, an artist RJ Davis introduced him to. "It gets me where I need to go," Hubert Davis said, sounding very much like a player who needs that pregame emotional energy.

"Deep down inside, he wishes he could still play," RJ Davis said. "He's a big-time Durk fan now. When we were in Brooklyn, Durk dropped a new album, and I sent it to Coach Davis right away. He always tells me he wants the clean version, but I tend to send him the explicit version because you get a better vibe off that."

Embracing that aggressive vibe helped change the season. "I want 17 guys in this locker room who are looking for a fight," Hubert Davis told his team. There would be no more questions about Carolina's toughness. Three days after the loss to Pitt, the Tar Heels went on the road and won at eventual ACC Tournament champion Virginia Tech, even on a raucous Saturday afternoon when the Hokies manufactured a Senior Day (they still had a home game remaining) just to amp their home crowd.

"Coach Davis changed our mentality," Love said. "We had been getting punched in the mouth and we didn't respond. He changed that, because he told us we were going to swing first. As soon as the ball was tipped, we were ready to be aggressive. We weren't trying to physically fight. But we weren't backing down from anybody." •

Caleb Love became the eighth
Tar Heel sophomore to score
600 points in a season.
PHOTO BY JEFFREY A. CAMARATI

Hubert Davis played against Mike Krzyzewski from 1988 to 1992 and went 2–1 against the Hall of Famer in 2022 as head coach.

PHOTO BY JEFFREY A. CAMARATI

Technical Tweaks

Carolina's in-season turnaround wasn't all team meetings and motivation.

The secondary break has been a staple of Tar Heel basketball since the Dean Smith era. The trailing big man knocking in a foul-line jumper has frustrated opponents for decades, just as a back screen for an alley-oop dunk worked for Michael Jordan just as flawlessly as it did for Vince Carter. Roy Williams remained fully committed to secondary for his entire tenure in Chapel Hill.

That philosophy continued—with some adjustments—in the early weeks of the Hubert Davis era. "We had tweaked it to fit our personnel," Davis said. "We didn't have Tony Bradley down there or Kennedy Meeks, where you just throw the ball into the post. We didn't even have the 2021 team, where we had four big guys. So we had already tweaked how we ran secondary."

Even more changes in personnel, however, caused a much more significant change. When the shorthanded Tar Heels attacked against Boston College and Notre Dame, driving to the basket and creating better scoring opportunities, the Carolina coaching staff realized the team was much more efficient playing a different style. This wasn't a small adjustment. It was essentially Tom Osborne ditching the wishbone at midseason to install a run-and-shoot attack.

"Secondary just wasn't working," Davis said. "We weren't getting anything out of it and we were wasting 10 or 15 seconds off the shot clock. We went up to play Boston College and we were down three guys, so I said just run 2K. We put two guys in the corner, two guys on the wings, and the five man set ball screens and rolled to the basket. And when we did it, I thought, 'Huh, this looks pretty good.'"

The Tar Heels demolished Boston College with that offense and used it on occasion in a road loss at Notre Dame. The true proof, though, came against noted defensive juggernaut Virginia, when the Tar Heels decimated the Cavaliers—a program that had dominated Carolina head-to-head in recent seasons—74–58 with a newly efficient offensive attack.

"If it can work against them, it can work against anybody," Davis told his assistants. "And by the end of the year, we weren't running any secondary at all."

It was an unprecedented switch to juggle the primary offense in midseason. But Carolina's players trusted their coach's experience. "At the end of the day, Coach Davis has played 12 years in the League, and he was successful," Caleb Love said. "We had no choice but to trust him. He's accomplished more than we have. And he told us we weren't getting anything out of secondary, that it wasn't benefiting this year's team. It might benefit next year's team or last year's team, but it just wasn't for us. For him to make that change and adjust the entire offense was amazing to me. The way he and this staff can put in certain plays on the fly and have them work right away is crazy. We were a team that was sinking. And he fixed it."

Starting guards Love and RJ Davis were largely excited about a change that would put the ball in their hands more often, creating driving opportunities and allowing them to make decisions. It was a tougher proposition for Armando Bacot, Carolina's marquee player whose game was built on receiving the ball close to the basket.

"I knew secondary was my bread and butter," Bacot said. "I wasn't used to setting screens and rolling. I knew it meant I was going to have to change my game a little. There were times I didn't get the ball when I was used to getting it, and I was in my feelings a little bit. I had to look in the mirror

Notre Dame · 78
UNC · 73

JANUARY 5, 2022

Armando Bacot had 17 re-bounds, which were then a career high, but Notre Dame made 13 three-pointers in the Irish's 78–73 win over the Tar Heels.

PHOTO BY MAGGIE HOBSON

Snow covered the campus and the temperature was in the 20s when Carolina traveled to South Bend to face Notre Dame, which was only 7–5 on the season but had won three in a row and a month earlier pinned a four-point loss on Kentucky.

The game turned out to be the only meeting of the season between the teams that would go on to tie for second place in the ACC standings with matching 15–5 league records and would combine for seven NCAA Tournament wins.

The Tar Heels were playing short-handed with Dawson Garcia out with a concussion and Justin McKoy and Kerwin Walton out for COVID safety protocols.

The Irish led by as many as 13, but Carolina rallied to a 67–66 lead behind Caleb Love's 13 second-half points and Armando Bacot's 21 points and career-high 17 rebounds. The lead was short-lived. Nate Laszewski hit a pair of threes and scored Notre Dame's next eight points to regain a five-point lead.

Carolina head coach Hubert Davis said before the game that a key to winning would be to limit dribble penetration and avoid the kickout pass to open three-point shooters, but the Irish made 13 threes and had 15 assists with just seven turnovers. On the other end, Notre Dame scored 19 points off 14 Tar Heel miscues.

RJ Davis had 19 points and five assists for Carolina, which shot 49.2 percent from the floor, its highest percentage in a loss all season.

Armando Bacot had career highs in points (29) and rebounds (22) in the home win over Virginia.

PHOTO BY ANTHONY SORBELLINI

UNC · 74
Virginia · 58

JANUARY 8, 2022

In a dominant season, Armando Bacot's best game of the 2021–22 season might have come in the 74–58 win over Virginia in the Smith Center.

Three days after a tough loss at Notre Dame, Bacot ensured a bounce-back win against UVA with his seventh consecutive double-double.

In snapping Carolina's seven-game losing streak to his home-state Cavaliers, the Richmond native set career highs in points (29), field goals (12), rebounds (22), and offensive rebounds (nine),

earning ACC and National Player of the Week honors a few days later.

Bacot was the first Tar Heel with a 20–20 game since 2016 and only the second to grab at least 20 rebounds in the Smith Center. In fact, while he was the first ACC player on any team to gather at least 22 rebounds since the 2016 ACC Tournament, Bacot's explosion against the Cavaliers was just one of an eventual five 20-rebound efforts for him during the 2021–22 season.

Brady Manek hit five three-pointers, dished out a career-high five assists, and scored 19 points. Caleb Love had five assists of his own, along with 16 points and four three-pointers. Bacot (with 29 points), Manek (19), and Love (16) combined to score 64 of UNC's 74 points.

The Tar Heels improved to 8–0 at home and hit 11 three-pointers as a team.

and realize that wasn't what was best for the team. This was going to force me to change my game, to make reads in the screen and roll, in a way that would help me at the next level. And it was going to help our team. Coach Davis revolutionized our offense in the middle of the season."

It was a high-risk strategy. Voluntarily taking Bacot off the low block seemed to weaken Carolina's strongest offensive asset. Neither Love nor Davis had yet proven they had the distributing mentality of a point guard. Sending six-foot-nine Brady Manek away from the basket was a move that ran counter to most of Carolina's basketball tradition, which was built on big men scoring high-percentage baskets close to the rim.

Hubert Davis wasn't worried.

"It wasn't scary to me, because the changes we were making weren't unknown to me," the head coach said. "We were using our guys in the wrong way. We were throwing Brady the ball and telling him to post up and hold his position. That's not him. He can finish around the basket, but he has to be on the move. He has to be setting a screen and rolling or getting the ball on a pick and pop.

RJ Davis and Caleb Love shared the Danny Green Most Improved Player Award.
PHOTO BY MAGGIE HOBSON

Brady Manek led the ACC in three-point percentage, one of four players six foot nine or taller ever to lead the league.

"I know this sounds weird, but that's the way I played when I was the JV coach. That's the way I love to play. I love scoring points in the paint. But my time with ESPN, my time in the NBA, and my time as the JV coach showed me there are other ways to get points in the paint. There are other ways of getting fouled and getting to the free throw line. We don't have big guys on the JV team. So that's the way I played. I knew what we were doing. And I knew it would work."

His players thrived under the new approach. Around the same time, RJ Davis assumed most of the ball-handling responsibilities. That left Love free to roam the perimeter as a scorer and relieved him of some point guard duties. The coaching staff continued to preach to him the importance of sharing the ball; the Tar Heels were still the best version of themselves when Love was drawing the defense by scoring and then finding teammates for easy baskets. Hubert Davis believed one of the most telling statistics of the year was that Carolina was an unbeaten 13–0 when Love had at least five assists and a pedestrian 16–10 when he did not.

Miami · 85
UNC · 57
JANUARY 18, 2022

Wake Forest · 98
UNC · 76
JANUARY 22, 2022

In what proved to be the most trying week of the season, Carolina lost consecutive mid-January games by 28 points at Miami and 22 at Wake Forest. The loss in Winston-Salem dropped the Tar Heels to 12–6 overall and 4–3 in league play. It marked the first time since 2001–02 that Carolina had lost consecutive games by 20 or more points.

UNC was coming off home wins over Virginia and Georgia Tech that earned Armando Bacot back-to-back ACC Player of the Week honors. But Bacot sprained his right thumb in the win over the Yellow Jackets and played tentatively in Coral Gables, while the Canes came out firing, building an 11-point lead in the first six minutes that ballooned quickly to 27 points by halftime. The Tar Heels shot only 22.6 percent from the floor in the first half, their worst 20 minutes of the season, and finished the contest six of 30 from three-point range.

Miami's Kameron McGusty, a teammate of Brady Manek's at Oklahoma, had 20 points, 10 rebounds, four assists, and four steals; Sam Waardenburg and Isaiah Wong both made five threes, and the Hurricanes harassed and hurried Carolina into 14 turnovers, which Miami remarkably converted into 30 points.

Four nights later, poor shooting by Carolina (33.3 percent from the floor, including six of 28 from three) and another high conversion of points off turnovers (21 points by Wake Forest off 11 UNC turnovers) spelled defeat again for the Tar Heels.

Jake LaRavia scored a career-best 31 points, Alondes Williams had 23, and Damari Monsanto came off the bench to hit three straight three-pointers midway through the second half to bust open the game for the Demon Deacons, who won for the 16th time in 20 games.

Manek led UNC with 22 points and RJ Davis added 18, but Carolina was whistled for 25 fouls, which led to 24 made free throws in 32 attempts for Wake Forest, including LaRavia's 12 of 15 shooting from the stripe.

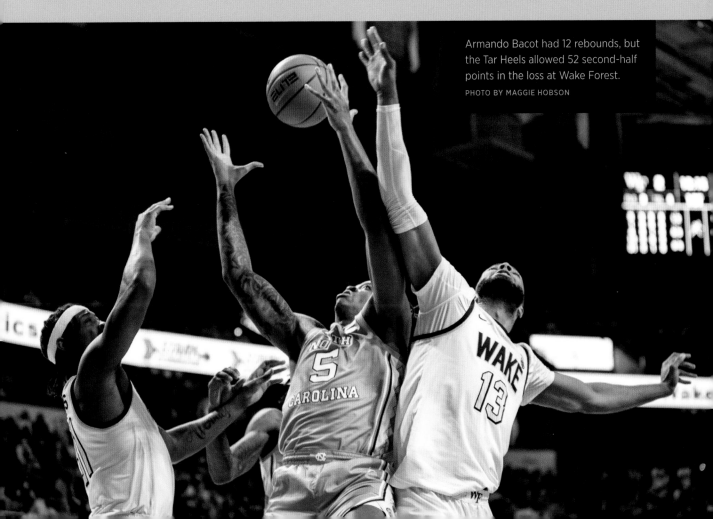

Armando Bacot had 12 rebounds, but the Tar Heels allowed 52 second-half points in the loss at Wake Forest.
PHOTO BY MAGGIE HOBSON

UNC · 78
Virginia Tech · 68
JANUARY 24, 2022

UNC · 58
Boston College · 47
JANUARY 26, 2022

UNC · 100
NC State · 80
JANUARY 29, 2022

RJ Davis was one of four Tar Heels to score in double figures in UNC's 100–80 win over NC State.

PHOTO BY ANTHONY SORBELLINI

Carolina had only two days after a blowout loss in Winston-Salem to rest and prepare for perhaps the most physically challenging portion of its schedule, playing three home games in six days. The Tar Heels badly needed a win after losing three of five ACC games.

Virginia Tech had been scheduled to visit the Smith Center in late December, but the game was postponed due to COVID-19 issues within the Hokies team.

The Tar Heels responded against the Hokies and won despite shooting under 40 percent as a team. Caleb Love led all scorers with 22 points, and Armando Bacot had another monster game on the boards, finishing with 14 points and 20 rebounds.

Two days later, UNC picked up its second win of the month against Boston College, 58–47. Carolina shot 29.1 percent from the floor, the lowest in school history in a win. Fortunately, the defense ensured the win by limiting the Eagles to 16 second-half points.

NC State made its annual visit to the Smith Center three days later, and the Tar Heels sent the Wolfpack home after a 100–80 drubbing. It was Carolina's 17th win over State in the last 19 meetings in Chapel Hill. UNC never trailed, cruising to a 25-point halftime lead after hitting 10 three-pointers and shooting 63 percent from the floor in the first half. Seven different Tar Heels hit a total of 15 threes in the game, the seventh-highest total in school history.

Bacot had yet another double-double, tallying 18 points, 13 rebounds, and six blocked shots. Love scored 21 and Brady Manek had 17 to lead the offensive blitz.

In six days, Carolina went from back-to-back 20-point losses to a three-game winning streak, proving its mettle in ways that would pay dividends late in the season.

Leaky Black hit multiple threes for the first time in 2021–22 in Carolina's home win over Virginia Tech.

PHOTO BY JEFFREY A. CAMARATI

But distributing the ball was not as instinctive to Love; while a traditional Carolina point guard might pass to set up his own scoring, what made Love so dangerous was his score-first mentality. Putting the ball in RJ Davis's hands allowed Love—like the rest of the team—to be more himself. Manek could be a floor-spacing perimeter sharpshooter. Davis and Love could get to the rim. Bacot was learning how to score on the move, which turned out to come naturally to him.

"The sets we were running weren't working," Manek said. "We kept missing a lot of small things. We always talked about how we weren't getting what we used to get off our secondary plays. But we weren't those teams. Those plays weren't working because of our personnel. What we switched into was a much better fit for our team, and that's why it worked."

The fifth starter, of course, was Leaky Black. And while he could do a little bit of everything—and became a reliable corner three-point shooter in the second half of the season—his primary function was as the team's defensive anchor. And while the Tar Heels didn't make the same pronounced adjustments on defense that they did on offense, a distinctly noticeable defensive change took place between December and April.

Opponents carved up Carolina early in the season by attacking them directly off the dribble. That didn't change as the season progressed. What changed was the way Carolina handled it.

Much of the early-season dribble penetration—by Kentucky's Sahvir Wheeler, for example, who scorched the Tar Heels with 26 points and eight assists in the Wildcats' 29-point win in December—was accomplished mostly by simply driving to the rim.

Hubert Davis was frustrated by the way the primary defender failed to handle that dribble penetration. But he was even more frustrated by the way the other four Tar Heels on the court failed to respond. On film, it sometimes looked like the other four defenders were unaware the penetration was even happening. They were too focused on their man, too committed to playing individual defense rather than team defense.

As the rotation shortened, the defensive communication became more intuitive. Players began to anticipate the defensive moves their teammates would make, and they responded accordingly. Roy Williams once described the very best defensive teams as "five players moving together on every pass." The late-season Tar Heels frequently resembled that description.

"When you're playing one-on-one defense, you're only worried about the guy you are guarding," Black said. "That's not how you are successful on defense. When you're playing five-on-five defense, everyone else has your back. If Caleb gets beat, Armando rotates over and helps clean it up, and I've got Mando's back on the box out. That's how we came together. That's the kind of defense you saw us play in the last month of the season."

Black's individual defense was stellar and earned him well-deserved national attention. But after Pittsburgh became the seventh opponent of the season to shoot at least 50 percent from the floor against Carolina, none of the final 13 opponents of the season reached that mark, and half the NCAA Tournament opponents didn't reach even 40 percent from the field.

The Tar Heel defense didn't always get much attention because it wasn't the brand that forces a barrage of turnovers. But the cohesive late-season iteration of Carolina was fully committed in the half-court.

"We started playing defense together instead of by ourselves," Manek said. "Watch the Duke game in Durham. Paolo [Banchero] would catch the ball out by the three-point line on the elbow. At the beginning of the year, if he did that, it would just be one on one, him against me. By the end of the year, I had him one on one, but Armando was under the goal, Leaky was in the gap, and RJ was staying right there. And if that made Paolo pass the ball, we were right there to contest the next guy. We forced guys to look at all five of us when thinking about making a move, and if they got in the paint, they were contested by several guys.

"Coach Davis helped make that happen by figuring out who he could trust and who we could stick with. On offense and defense, he did what would work best for us, and what he thought would make us most successful. That's how we were successful." •

In Carolina's victory at Cameron Indoor Stadium, Paolo Banchero led Duke with 23 points, but tough team defense held the Duke star to 11 of 26 field goals.

PHOTO BY MAGGIE HOBSON

Leaky Black was solid on both ends of the floor in UNC's overtime win at Louisville in early February.

PHOTO BY MAGGIE HOBSON

The Maturation of Leaky Black

No player on Carolina's 2022 roster went through a more dramatic transformation than Leaky Black. The Concord native began the season with a career shooting percentage below 40 percent, and his Carolina career had largely been defined to that point more by what he hadn't done than what he had done.

Black entered school in the fall of 2018 with Nassir Little and Coby White, two players who enjoyed standout freshman seasons and then departed for the NBA. Black's progress was more gradual. He'd spent most of his life as a point guard, even after growing to six foot seven. But the Tar Heels always had someone in that position, so Black played most of his minutes on the wing. The public was also unaware of how problematic a series of injuries had been to Black's progress, especially a nagging ankle injury that limited his running, jumping, and lateral movement. The version of Black Tar Heel fans saw in his first three years in the program was often one who was playing hurt.

Black was not a natural fit on the wing, and his three-point percentage dropped to 22.2 as a junior, when he started all but one game but also saw his minutes, scoring, and rebounding numbers drop just slightly. Roy Williams always believed Black could have a Jackie Manuel brand of impact if he fully committed himself to defending, using that lanky frame and wingspan to make life difficult for opposing shooters.

But as with many players, it was tough for Black to fully give himself over to an intangible type of role. No one signs to play college basketball for North Carolina thinking, "Hopefully I can be the guy they don't rely on for scoring."

It wasn't until Manuel himself joined Hubert Davis's staff that Black fully understood what that kind of role could mean. When Manuel won a national championship with the 2005 Tar Heels, Black was only six years old. For all he knew, Manuel's journey had been easy. The introverted Black also needed time for his relationship with Manuel to develop.

Director of team and player development Jackie Manuel and Leaky Black developed a close relationship. PHOTO BY MAGGIE HOBSON

Black's senior season began disappointingly when his teammates voted Armando Bacot, Caleb Love, and RJ Davis to be team captains. Black knew his personality made him an unusual fit for the role, as he was typically very quiet off the court. But he had hoped his on-court leadership might earn him a few votes.

"It hurt," Black said. "I knew people would see I hadn't been elected captain and start asking questions. When Coach told us the outcome of the voting, he made it clear that it was selected by the players. The first thing that went through my head was 'Some of these guys didn't vote for me. Somebody didn't believe in me.'

"I don't think I ever really said anything about it at the time or during the season, because I didn't want anyone to know it bothered me. If anything, I wanted to make sure I was still talking in practice and still trying to be a leader."

The regular season began just four days later, leaving Black in the uncomfortable position of still wondering about his role on the team while also trying to contribute on the court. He had played only sporadically in Carolina's scrimmage at Florida and knew his starting spot might be in question if the Tar Heels decided to play with a bigger lineup.

UNC · 90
Louisville · 83 (OT)

FEBRUARY 1, 2022

The Tar Heels faced Louisville at the KFC Yum! Center with a 7-3 record in league play. The Cardinals were just days removed from dismissing head coach Chris Mack and placing assistant coach Mike Pegues in charge of the program on an interim basis.

The Tar Heels came into the KFC Yum! Center 7–3 in league play, while the Cardinals were just days removed from dismissing their head coach and placing assistant coach Mike Pegues in charge of the program on an interim basis.

Carolina head coach Hubert Davis emphasized taking care of the ball after UNC committed 30 more turnovers than its opponents in its first six road games and allowed 51 points off turnovers at Miami and Wake Forest.

RJ Davis led UNC with 10 first-half points in a back-and-forth game in which the Tar Heels led by one point at the break. Carolina began the second half on a 19–10 run to open a 55–45 lead with 12:35 to play. But the Cardinals hit four straight three-pointers—three by El Ellis, who scored 20 second-half points—over the next four minutes to give Louisville a 57–55 advantage.

The game remained close throughout the remainder of regulation with Armando Bacot giving UNC a 74–72 lead with 49 seconds left and Ellis tying the game on a steal and drive with 15 seconds to play. RJ Davis's layup with two seconds left was blocked to send the game to overtime.

Caleb Love, who had committed a costly turnover late in regulation, began the extra period with a three-pointer and scored eight of Carolina's 16 points in overtime. Leaky Black, who hit a season-high three three-pointers and scored a season-best 13 points, gave Carolina the lead for good at 84–81 with a three from the corner.

Brady Manek led all five starters in double figures with 24 points (the bench did not score); Bacot had 19 points and a career-high-tying 22 rebounds; and Davis and Love combined for 34 points and 11 assists.

The teams combined for 27 three-pointers, but the key stats were that Carolina committed only 10 turnovers; outscored the Cardinals, 13–10, in points off turnovers; had 18 assists on 31 Tar Heel field goals; and held the home team to 40 percent shooting.

RJ Davis hit four threes and had five assists and 18 points at Louisville.

PHOTO BY MAGGIE HOBSON

Duke · 87
UNC · 67

FEBRUARY 5, 2022

When Mike Krzyzewski made his final appearance as Duke head coach in the Smith Center, the Tar Heel faithful were ready. Carolina fans showed up early and created the rowdiest Smith Center environment of the season . . . but only for a few minutes.

The Blue Devils quieted the crowd quickly, jumping out to a 19–5 lead in the first five minutes and leading by 23 at the midway point of the first half.

Carolina eventually rallied and cut the lead to 11 by halftime, only to allow Duke to start the second period with a 12–0 run and build the advantage right back

to 23. The Tar Heels never got closer than 16 points the rest of the way, as Duke shot 58 percent from the floor in a dominant team effort.

Brady Manek was the lone bright spot for Carolina. He scored 14 of UNC's 28 first-half points, finishing with 21 after hitting six of 10 three-pointers.

Meanwhile, Duke shot 55 percent from the floor in the first half, 60 percent in the second, and 58 percent for the game while drubbing Carolina on the backboards, 40–24. AJ Griffin led the way with 27 points, hitting 11 of 17 shots.

In the face of a disappointing home loss, Hubert Davis, as always, chose to remain positive.

"There are only two choices," Davis told his team after the game. "Stay down on the mat and whine and complain and point fingers and make excuses. Or get up off the mat. Those are the only two choices. I'm already off the mat. My hope and expectation is everyone else in this locker room will do the same."

Brady Manek made six three-pointers and scored 21 in the 20-point home loss to Duke.

PHOTO BY JEFFREY A. CAMARATI

Leaky Black earned All-ACC Defensive Team honors and was a candidate for National Defensive Player of the Year.

PHOTO BY JACK MORTON

He played 21 minutes in the opener against Loyola and 19 in a win over Brown, earning praise from the coaches for his defense. But the dismal two-game stretch at Miami and Wake Forest saw him play just a combined 27 minutes. To that point, his senior season wasn't much different from his first three years; there were some flashes, including 10 points in a home win over Virginia Tech and a pair of defensive lock-downs of Georgia Tech's high-scoring Michael Devoe. But he was confused about his role and sometimes felt his minutes didn't match his effort. For someone who keeps most of his conflict bottled up inside, it was a trying situation.

"I felt like Coach Davis didn't believe in me," Black said. "What I've realized now is that I didn't believe in myself. At the beginning, I was thinking a lot about the captain stuff and my minutes. You hear all this stuff from your family and you start to wonder if you would be better off somewhere else. What I decided was that I had to get better. I had to find a way to stay on the court and make it so that everyone knew we were a better team with me out there. That's when my defense stepped up."

Black's effort eventually earned him All-ACC Defensive Team honors, Carolina's first such selection since 2016. He was sensational in three separate games against Virginia Tech's Hunter Cattoor. He blanketed Duke's Paolo Banchero in Chapel Hill, then switched to the Blue Devils' AJ Griffin in the remaining two contests against Duke and largely erased him from the games. He was similarly successful on defense against Syracuse's Buddy Boeheim and NC State's Dereon Seabron.

In the NCAA Tournament, Carolina identified the opponent's best wing scorer and latched Black onto him. He limited Marquette's leading scorer, Justin Lewis, to just two for 15 from the field. Baylor's Matthew Mayer managed just three for eight. UCLA's Jaime Jaquez went only five for 18. Doug Edert from Saint Peter's had been one of the primary stories of the NCAA Tournament. Then he ran into Black and went zero for five.

"I never once looked at the bracket," Black said of his defensive consistency. "I didn't even watch the tournament other than our games. I just looked at who we had to play. That buildup of Doug Edert from Saint Peter's? I had no idea who he was, and that's not meant as a slap at him, because I didn't pay attention to anybody. I just knew he had a mustache and everyone loved him. I didn't see anything other than what I saw when we were preparing to play them."

Bacot was consistently piling up double-doubles, but Black's game was just as consistent on the defensive side. He was the basketball equivalent of having a lockdown corner in football who completely eliminates one receiver from the game. Black's man simply never had a quality performance. The consistency was remarkable, especially given the struggles Black had experienced during his Carolina career. He credited Manuel for helping him strengthen his mental toughness and helping him cope with what was sometimes a physically debilitating case of anxiety.

Just as Courtney Banghart had predicted, Manuel's knowledge of people had a powerful impact on the Tar Heels. Manuel was sometimes known as "Sergeant Jackie," capable of sternly rebuking a player who kept a dirty locker. Because he wasn't one of Carolina's three official bench assistant coaches, he was not permitted to coach during practice. But after practice, he occasionally admonished players—in a harsher tone than some might have expected from an individual generally considered one of the kindest people in the program—who were ignoring a coach's direction or giving half-hearted effort.

Leaky Black had eight assists in the NCAA first-round win over Marquette.
PHOTO BY MAGGIE HOBSON

UNC · 79
Clemson · 77

FEBRUARY 8, 2022

When the Tar Heels lined up to play at Clemson, a year removed from a 13-point loss in Littlejohn Coliseum, they faced the possibility of a first-ever three-game losing streak to the Tigers. In the 2021 defeat, no starter scored in double figures and UNC committed 10 more turnovers than their opponent.

The 2022 road trip didn't start much better as the Tigers jumped out to a 19-8 lead in the first 10 minutes. Armando Bacot sparked a 13-2 run by the Tar Heels to draw even at 21, and the visitors took a five-point lead into halftime after a three by RJ Davis and a dunk by Bacot, who scored 15 first-half points.

Leaky Black began the second half scoring UNC's first six points, and Brady Manek buried a three for a nine-point lead, but the Tigers quickly pulled within a point.

The game, which featured 10 lead changes and seven ties in the second half alone, remained within three points for all but a single possession over the final 11:41. Black hit a three to give Carolina a 72–68 lead, but Clemson's PJ Hall answered with a three of his own.

The Tigers took a 75–74 lead on a layup by Hall with 71 seconds to play before Caleb Love hit a three with 36 seconds to go to put the Tar Heels ahead by two.

Hall converted inside again to even the game at 77. Following a UNC time-out with 15 seconds on the clock, Love drove the ball down the lane and swung a pass to a cutting Manek, who laid the ball in the basket with 3.1 seconds left for the win.

Bacot tied Hall for scoring honors with 24 points and added 10 rebounds and three assists. All five Carolina starters scored in double figures, including Davis, who had six assists and no turnovers.

The Tar Heels overcame 14 turnovers and Clemson's 19 of 21 free throws by shooting 50 percent from the floor (60.7 percent over the final 20 minutes).

Leaky Black became one of the premier perimeter defenders in college basketball.

PHOTO BY MAGGIE HOBSON

That worked for some players. But Manuel clearly saw that working with Black required a different approach, and he was equipped to provide it.

"Jackie Manuel started praying with me before the games," Black said. "After every prayer, he'd say, 'You're going to do great.' That really gave me the confidence and the ability to relax. Without it, my anxiety started to take over. I'd start getting jittery and my arms would tense up, they'd be going numb, and I'd shoot terribly."

Black discussed his challenges with anxiety openly with the media after making a key three-pointer in the win at Louisville. He hadn't even planned to make the revelation. With press conferences still conducted over Zoom due to the pandemic, he didn't have to face a sea of unnerving microphones. Instead, he just looked into the computer screen and started talking.

"That wasn't the plan," Black said. "We didn't really have a plan. I just knew that Jackie was praying with me to have a great year and a great day, and once he started doing that, everything changed. Admitting the problem and embracing it instead of running from a situation makes it so much easier."

Carolina's win at Clemson was one of seven conference road wins for the Tar Heels.

Black's defense, which helped propel the storybook postseason run, endeared him to Tar Heel fans across the country. But he noticed an even bigger change on campus, where suddenly he was regularly being stopped by fellow students.

That's just life for a high-profile starter in a winning college basketball town. Frequently, though, these students wanted to talk about something other than basketball.

"It used to be that when I was walking to class people wanted to ask for a picture or an autograph," Black said. "Now they want to talk about how I changed their life, about how me using my platform to talk about therapy and treatment touched their lives. It's completely changed how I look at being a Carolina basketball player. They aren't just fans. It's part of a community, and we're all in this together."

It turned into a full-circle moment for the player who early in the season had questioned if he was meant to be at Carolina and by April was making the decision to come back for a fifth year. He'd spent early practices wondering why his teammates didn't respect him enough to elect him a captain. And by the NCAA Tournament, those same teammates were turning to him for advice that helped the Tar Heels advance in the postseason.

In a close regional semifinal against UCLA in the regional semifinal—a high-level offensive battle that was quietly perhaps the most well-played game of the entire tournament run—Hubert Davis pulled a frustrated Brady Manek with 8:38 to go to let the Oklahoma native collect himself. That forced the Tar Heels to juggle defensive assignments. Faced with guarding the talented Jaime Jaquez, Caleb Love immediately knew what to do: he went to Black and asked him the best way to defend Jaquez. "Get into him and make him put it on the floor," the senior said.

Jaquez missed a pair of jumpers and did not score with Love guarding him, as the Tar Heels trimmed three points off the UCLA lead with Manek on the bench.

"Leaky is a leader," Love said. "I learned a lot from him this whole year. What you have to understand about him is that his leadership is going to be by example. You don't have to make a bunch of shots to be a leader. If you come in and work hard, your teammates will see that and follow suit. We see that with Leaky, and that's why we can follow his lead." •

Senior Leaky Black and graduate student Brady Manek became roommates and tremendous leaders on and off the court.

PHOTO BY JEFFREY A. CAMARATI

Armando Bacot is one of eight Tar Heels in history to average a career double-double in points and rebounds.

PHOTO BY ANTHONY SORBELLINI

Bacot led UNC in scoring, rebounding, field goal percentage, and blocked shots for the second consecutive season.

PHOTO BY MAGGIE HOBSON

Bacot's Breakout Season

The win at Louisville was one of three games in which Bacot had a career-high 22 rebounds.

PHOTO BY MAGGIE HOBSON

Armando Bacot vividly remembered the moment when his Carolina basketball career changed.

It was the end-of-season meeting after his freshman campaign as a Tar Heel. He'd enjoyed a solid season, starting all 32 games, playing the fourth-most minutes on the team, scoring 9.6 points per game, and grabbing 8.2 rebounds per contest. Those were very respectable numbers for a freshman.

So Bacot was feeling pretty good about himself when he walked into Roy Williams's office for his exit meeting. Williams asked him to evaluate himself on a scale of one to 10 on his love, passion, and effort for the game.

"I'd give myself a six or seven," Bacot said.

Williams, always a stern grader, replied, "I'd give you a four."

Williams's then lieutenant Hubert Davis was also in the room. He didn't hesitate. "I'd give you a one," he told Bacot. "You are so gifted. Things come very easily for you academically, socially, and with basketball. Because of that, you don't give your best all the time. Until that changes, none of the dreams you have will ever come true."

Bacot walked into the meeting feeling like a star and walked out wondering if he could actually play college basketball at a high level. He knew the Tar Heels were bringing in two standout freshman post players, Walker Kessler and Day'Ron Sharpe, who were not coming to Chapel Hill with the intention of sitting on the bench. Even a self-administered grade of six or seven wasn't going to be enough to earn playing time next season.

"I still remember driving home after that meeting," Bacot said. "I was very emotional. I was crying. But that meeting changed my life. That's when I started to take this seriously and really understand what kind of work was required to play at this level. That was the turning point of how I carry myself and my entire basketball career. It fueled me to get to this point. I had to make a decision about what I wanted to be, and I decided I want to go out and compete every single day.

Armando Bacot secured 20 rebounds in the home win over Virginia Tech, one of five games with 20 or more, which tied the UNC record.

Armando Bacot: A Historic Season

CAREER

- One of two Tar Heels in the last 50 seasons and eight all-time to average a double-double in points and rebounds
- Rebound average of 10.0 is the sixth highest by a Tar Heel and is the highest since Sean May from 2002 to 2005
- Joins Billy Cunningham and Antawn Jamison as the only Tar Heels with 1,000 rebounds in three seasons
- Has 49 double-doubles, the third most in UNC history, behind Cunningham's 60 and Jamison's 51

2021–22

- Led Carolina in scoring (16.3), rebounding (13.1), field goal percentage (.569), and blocks (65), becoming the first Tar Heel to lead the team in those categories in consecutive seasons
- One of three players to make both the All-ACC Academic Team and All-ACC first team
- Earned All–NCAA Tournament honors in the Final Four and East Regional, where he was also the Most Outstanding Player
- Third-team CBS Sports and USA Today All-America, leading vote-getter on the All-ACC first team, second in ACC Player of the Year voting, and recipient of UNC's Athletic Director's Scholar-Athlete Award
- Earned second straight Dean Smith Most Valuable Player Award
- Won UNC's Rammy for Best Male Athlete in 2021–22
- First college basketball player with six double-doubles in one NCAA Tournament

- Tied the NCAA single-season record with 31 double-doubles (with Navy's David Robinson in 1985–86)
- Second-most rebounds (99) ever in an NCAA Tournament and the most since 1954
- Fourth-most rebounds in a season in ACC history and the first player with at least 500 since 1956
- Single-season Tar Heel record with 511 rebounds, 95 more than the previous record set by Brice Johnson in 2015–16
- Tied the UNC record for 20-rebound games in a season with five and set the school record with 32 games in double figures
- Rebounding average (13.1) was the highest by a Tar Heel since 1964–65
- Led the ACC in all games by 4.94 rebounds per game (the difference between second place and 20th was 2.1 per game)
- Averaged 14.1 rebounds in league play, the most since Wake Forest's Tim Duncan averaged 14.9 in 1996–97
- Broke Duncan's previous ACC double-double record (29 in 1996–97) and Johnson's UNC record (23 in 2015–16)
- Led the nation in double-doubles and was second in offensive rebounding (4.2), third in rebounding, and 23rd in field goal percentage (.569)
- Led the ACC in rebounding, offensive rebounding, and double-doubles and was second in field goal percentage, fifth in blocks, and seventh in scoring
- Scored in double figures 34 times with 20 or more points 11 times
- Led Carolina in scoring a team-high 14 times

- Averaged 15.3 points and 16.5 rebounds in six NCAA Tournament games
- Shattered UNC's NCAA Tournament single-season record for rebounds with 99
- Tied the UNC record for rebounds in an NCAA Tournament game with 22 versus Saint Peter's and became the only Tar Heel with two 20-rebound NCAA Tournament games when he had 21 versus Duke in the national semifinals
- His 21 rebounds versus Duke were the most by any player in the Final Four since 2003 and were the most ever by a Tar Heel in 21 national semifinals
- Became the 12th player with 21 or more rebounds in a Final Four game—the list includes Naismith Hall of Famers Bill Russell (twice), Elvin Hayes, Lew Alcindor, Bill Walton, Elgin Baylor, and Artis Gilmore
- Had 10 straight double-doubles from the Furman through Virginia Tech games, the most by a Tar Heel since Cunningham had 10 in a row in 1964–65 and tying the fourth-longest streak by a Tar Heel
- Thirteen straight games with 10 or more rebounds was the third-longest streak in UNC history
- The only three-time ACC Player of the Week in the league in 2021–22
- First Tar Heel to score 29 or more points in consecutive games since Tyler Hansbrough in 2008
- First Tar Heel with at least 29 points and 12 rebounds in consecutive games since Charlie Scott in 1970
- Career highs in points (29), field goals (12), rebounds (22), and offensive rebounds (9) in January win over Virginia; also had 22 rebounds at Louisville and versus Saint Peter's

Armando Bacot earned ACC Player of the Week honors for the second straight week after his 29-point performance versus Georgia Tech.

PHOTO BY JEFFREY A. CAMARATI

Bacot had 17 points and 18 rebounds in the Senior Night win over Syracuse.

Bacot was excited when Davis was named head coach. "I've had a relationship with him since the ninth grade," he noted. "He's going to tell me the truth, and he wants to make me the absolute best I can be."

Bacot's drive is matched by his interest in the Carolina basketball record book. It struck him in December that he didn't know who held the Carolina single-game scoring record. So he inquired about it and was surprised to find out that it belongs to Bobby Lewis, who scored 49 points against Florida State in 1965, a record that has stood for over half a century.

Even an ambitious Bacot thought that mark was probably out of reach. But his research did reveal a few other records he thought were attainable.

"I started to look at my stats after I had back-to-back 29-point games," he said of his January performances at the Smith Center against Virginia and Georgia Tech. "That's around the time I reached averaging a double-double. That was one of my goals. Then I started looking at my rebounding numbers. Earlier in my career, I had always told the coaches I thought I could average 12 or 13 rebounds per game. At that point, I was getting eight or nine rebounds in fewer minutes. Once I started putting up those numbers this season, I was like, 'See, this is exactly what I was saying.'"

When Davis made the in-season switch to an offense that relied less on the secondary break, he did it knowing that Bacot would be hesitant about a change that seemed to lessen the importance of some of his best qualities. But the offense Davis wanted to utilize more frequently was actually a very good fit for their junior center.

Davis also knew that Bacot's intelligence would allow him to understand the goals of the change and how it fit with his game. Bacot is a Dean's List student who can often be found in the front row of his classes at Kenan-Flagler Business School with some of the brightest minds at the university. (He regularly discusses the stock market with friends around the university.)

"Armando is incredible finishing around the basket on the move," the Tar Heel head coach said. "Now we had spacing, now we had movement, and we were able to get him the ball closer to the basket on the move, and it just opened him up. We weren't just dribbling the ball and throwing it to him on the block. He excelled coming off screens or with dribble handoffs or guys helping up the land and then we're able to throw it to him."

Armando Bacot was Carolina's Dean Smith Most Valuable Player for the second consecutive season.
PHOTO BY MAGGIE HOBSON

Carolina stumbled at home, losing to Pitt before reeling off a season-best six-game winning streak.

PHOTO BY ANTHONY SORBELLINI

Pittsburgh · 76
UNC · 67

FEBRUARY 16, 2022

The most inexplicable of Carolina's 39 games was undoubtedly its 76–67 loss to Pittsburgh on February 16 in the Smith Center.

Carolina had won six of its previous seven games to sit at 10–4 in ACC play, one game behind Duke and Notre Dame for the top spot in the conference. The Panthers were 10–16 overall, 5–10 in the ACC, although they had defeated Florida State and NC State in their previous two games.

The first half was virtually all Pitt, as the Panthers broke a 12–12 tie with a 17–2

run en route to a 40–23 lead. The visitors made 15 of 25 from the floor in the half, including six of nine from three-point range. Carolina hit on just eight of 29 (27.6 percent, UNC's second-lowest percentage ever in a half in the Smith Center) and committed 10 turnovers, which the Panthers converted into 20 points.

Pitt's lead grew to 21 in the second half before the Tar Heels made a late run to pull within single digits with 2:28 to play and to within six at 69–63 after a Brady Manek basket with 1:50 remaining.

The comeback came to an end after a turnover and John Hugley basket with 90 seconds to go. Ithiel Horton made all five of his three-point attempts and had 19 points, and Hugley added 18 points for the Panthers.

Pitt didn't win again in 2021–22, dropping its next five games after the win over the Tar Heels, while Carolina went on to victories in 11 of its final 13 games.

Armando Bacot was the leading vote-getter on the All-ACC first team and was second in Player of the Year balloting.

The numbers were undeniable. In the 25 games beginning with the win over Virginia, Bacot had 21 double-doubles. He had three games scoring at least 25 points and five games with at least 20 rebounds. In the first two and a half years of his Tar Heel career, he hadn't reached that scoring or rebounding milestone in any game.

One of the coaches charged with fostering Bacot's development was assistant Sean May. As a former Carolina post player who has his jersey in the Smith Center rafters for his legendary performance during the 2005 national championship run and played several years in the NBA, May had a unique understanding of the progress Bacot needed to make. The first-year Tar Heel assistant coach—who had been on staff in an administrative role for six seasons and is the only Carolina player in the last 50 years to average a double-double in his UNC career—began preparing clip tapes after every game. The videos were focused exclusively on Bacot. Sometimes they were big baskets or other things he did correctly. Just as often, they were areas where he could improve, even if it was as simple as how aggressively he rolled to the rim after setting a screen.

Bacot soaked in the instruction just as he did in his business school classes. "It allowed me to visualize what [May] was talking about," he said. "It's one thing to tell me in practice. It's another to do it on video, where I can just focus on myself. That was huge for me."

Armando Bacot set the UNC single-season rebound record with 511.

PHOTO BY MAGGIE HOBSON

UNC · 65
Virginia Tech · 57

FEBRUARY 19, 2022

Only three days after one of the season's lowest points, Carolina faced a difficult test when it visited Virginia Tech for a nationally televised contest that felt like an old-school, Saturday afternoon ACC battle.

It wasn't necessarily a pretty game, but it was one of the biggest road wins of the season in a raucous environment, and it significantly boosted UNC's NCAA Tournament credentials.

The Tar Heels held Tech to a season-low scoring total at home and emerged with a 65–57 win behind strong efforts from Caleb Love and Armando Bacot.

Love scored a game-high 21 points while dishing out a season-high seven assists with just two turnovers. Bacot posted his 20th double-double of the season, with 12 points, 15 rebounds, and five blocked shots.

Emergent defensive star Leaky Black provided a boost by holding Tech's Hunter Cattoor, who entered the game hitting over 45 percent of his three-point attempts, to just one of six from behind the arc and two of seven overall. The Hokies were just five for 26 as a team from three-point range.

At the time that Carolina made the offensive switch, many ACC observers were already touting Wake Forest's Alondes Williams for the league's Player of the Year award. And while the Demon Deacon transfer from Oklahoma did have an outstanding year, the early publicity eventually became somewhat of a self-fulfilling prophecy. Williams received the honor even though his team and individual accomplishments were eventually less impressive than what Bacot achieved.

The Tar Heel big man ultimately tied an NCAA record set by David Robinson 35 years ago with 31 double-doubles during the season. That was a record Bacot didn't even know existed until the final weeks of the season. His goals—including getting his jersey in the Smith Center rafters, an honor that follows selection as the ACC Player of the Year—will be even higher next season. After all, he knows the record book even more intimately now that he appears in several prominent places.

"I like setting goals and then competing with myself to see if I can do it," Bacot said. "I first wanted Brice Johnson's season record for double-doubles at Carolina. Now I want the longest streak of double-doubles." To get there, Bacot will need to extend his current streak of eight straight for another 33 games, which would top Billy Cunningham's record of 40 straight.

It's just one of the things that motivated Bacot to return for his senior season. "I'm one of those guys that breaking records motivates me," he acknowledged. "And there are still some things I think I can do at Carolina." •

Ryan McAdoo, Leaky Black, and Brady Manek were honored as part of Carolina's Senior Night ceremonies. PHOTO BY JEFFREY A. CAMARATI

UNC · 88
Syracuse · 79 (OT)

FEBRUARY 28, 2022

Carolina came into Senior Night on an impressive three-game win streak with victories at Virginia Tech, over Louisville, and at NC State. The Orange were 9–9 in the ACC but loaded with veteran players and outstanding three-point shooters.

In the end, the Tar Heels pulled out an 88–79 win in overtime. Brady Manek, playing his final game in the Smith Center, scored 22 points; Armando Bacot had 17 points and 18 rebounds; Leaky Black had seven assists and blocked three shots; and RJ Davis hit five threes.

But it was mainly the late-game heroics of Caleb Love that sent Carolina home with the victory. Love scored 14 of his 21 points in the final seven and a half minutes, including Carolina's final six points of regulation and eight of 15 in overtime.

Love had made two of his first 14 shots from the floor before dropping in a three-pointer with 2:29 to play in the second half for a 70–69 lead. With eight seconds remaining in regulation and Syracuse back on top by a point, Love nailed another three for a 73–71 lead.

Syracuse raced up the floor and sent the game to extra time on a jumper by Joe Girard III with two seconds left.

The overtime was all Carolina. Manek began an 8–0 run with a jumper and Love and Davis followed with threes to pull away. The Tar Heels followed a second half in which they made only 26.5 percent from the floor by knocking in five of six shots in overtime.

Carolina overcame a 36-point effort by Cole Swider, who scored 21 first-half points and went seven for 11 from beyond the arc.

The victory clinched a double bye for the Tar Heels in the 2022 ACC Tournament.

Carolina clinched a double bye in the ACC Tournament with a win over Syracuse as Caleb Love scored 14 points in the final seven minutes. PHOTO BY JEFFREY A. CAMARATI

Bacot was fifth in the ACC in blocked shots with a career-best 65, three more than he blocked in his first two years combined.

PHOTO BY JEFFREY A. CAMARATI

RJ Davis was one of four Tar Heels to score 20 points at Duke, a feat UNC accomplished for the first time in program history.
PHOTO BY MAGGIE HOBSON

The Power of Belief

Carolina talked little all week about strategy and focused instead on taking the fight to the Blue Devils.

PHOTO BY MAGGIE HOBSON

Carolina finished its home schedule on the last day of February with a win over Syracuse. As the Tar Heels eyed the regular-season finale at Duke the next Saturday, they had almost a whole week to notice something about the chatter surrounding the rivalry matchup: absolutely no one gave even the slightest consideration to the idea that the Tar Heels might win the game.

The national expectation seemed to be that Carolina was there primarily to play the Washington Generals role for a rousing send-off for Mike Krzyzewski in his final game at Cameron Indoor Stadium. In the days leading up to the game, one of the many media entities producing content for the game had a meeting regarding its plans for coverage of the numerous Krzyzewski-centric ceremonies. Someone present at the meeting asked a very simple question: "What happens if Carolina wins the game?"

Hubert Davis's relaxed demeanor helped his team maintain their poise in hostile environments such as Cameron Indoor Stadium.
PHOTO BY MAGGIE HOBSON

The question stopped the meeting cold. No one had even considered that possibility. They quickly brushed off the far-fetched idea of a Tar Heel victory and continued with their Duke programming.

"We were an afterthought," Hubert Davis said. "It helped me because I poked at that with the team. It helped me focus them. I understood that they beat us badly in the first game. But it ticked me off that no one ever factored in that we were involved in the game, too."

"It pissed us off," Armando Bacot agreed. "We were a team that fed the whole year off what people said we couldn't do. We felt disrespected that no one thought we could win."

Davis amplified that disrespect with his tone within minutes of beating Syracuse, pacing with fury that his team wasn't being seen as Duke's equal. The Blue Devils still had a game to play the following evening before they could focus on the Tar Heels, but Davis was already game-ready.

"I'm going to tell you something," he said that night. "We are not going over there for a party. We are not going over there to be part of some festivities. We are going over there to play a game. And we're going to play."

UNC · 94
Duke · 81

MARCH 5, 2022

It was a game for the ages, but not as most had planned. ESPN and the ACC Network offered multichannel coverage before, during, and after the game, including carrying the postgame observance live on both networks. Almost all the focus was on Duke and the buildup to a game flanked by two elaborately planned ceremonies honoring Mike Krzyzewski. But the Tar Heels emerged from Cameron Indoor Stadium with a convincing 94–81 victory, tying for second place in the ACC standings in the process.

Showing as much grit as it had all season, Carolina played four players for 38 minutes or more and did not substitute once after halftime despite the charged, intense action on the court and the warm temperatures in the building.

After a tight first 20 minutes that ended in a two-point lead for the Blue Devils, the Tar Heels blitzed Duke after halftime, hitting 59.4 percent of their shots from the floor, including four of seven from three-point range, and outscoring Duke 55–40.

It was the first time an unranked Carolina team had beaten a top-five Duke team in Durham since 1990.

For the first time in program history, four Tar Heels scored 20 or more points in a game: Armando Bacot (23), Caleb Love (22), RJ Davis (21), and Brady Manek (20). Bacot hit 10 of 11 shot attempts and was unstoppable in the high-post pick play with Davis, who drove the lane with abandon, hit nine of 16 field goals, and controlled the pace in one of his best games of the season. Manek added 11 rebounds for his third double-double as a Tar Heel, and Love had at least 20 for the third time in four career games against Duke.

Carolina played with veteran poise throughout and made 19 of 22 free throws as a team, including 12 of 12 by Love. The Tar Heels then headed to the ACC Tournament having won 11 of their last 13 games and earning the no. 3 seed.

Leaky Black helped Carolina outscore the Blue Devils by 15 points in the second half in the win at Cameron. PHOTO BY MAGGIE HOBSON

RJ Davis's three-pointer just before the half cut Duke's lead to just two points. PHOTO BY MAGGIE HOBSON

The week's tone in practice mirrored Davis's laser focus. The Smith Center speakers blared the Duke anthem "Everytime We Touch" before practice, and equipment manager Shane Parrish took to humming the tune anytime a player was around. Davis whistled practice to a stop during one drill when the Tar Heel starters let the scout team offense complete a pass too easily. "No!" he barked. "It is not going down like that. I'm telling you right now. That is not how we are playing on Saturday."

While the rest of the country was completely focused on Duke, the Tar Heels were building a quiet confidence. All week, Davis emphasized one of his most frequent sayings, drawing from Proverbs 4:25, as the Thought for the Day at the top of each day's practice plan: Keep your eyes straight ahead; ignore all sideshow distractions.

RJ Davis and Bacot were chatting in the Smith Center at midweek. Davis looked at his older teammate and said, "I really feel like we could pull this off. I think we're going to win at Duke and beat Coach K in his last game at Duke."

A few weeks later, RJ Davis was asked what gave him such a sense of confidence.

Leaky Black's layup gave UNC a four-point lead with five minutes to play.

PHOTO BY MAGGIE HOBSON

Puff Johnson helped Carolina win at Duke for the second year in a row.

PHOTO BY MAGGIE HOBSON

"When Coach Davis stopped practice and told us we weren't going to play that way, that set the whole tone," he said. "He let us know right away that it wasn't going to be easy. The way we lost to them the first time was embarrassing. I told myself that was not going to happen again. We had nothing to lose. The pressure wasn't on us. I felt deep down in my heart that we were going to win the game."

The Tar Heels loaded the team bus in a downstairs tunnel on the afternoon of the game. Hubert Davis waited until everyone was on board. Then he hopped up the stairs and faced his team. He had just one message for them.

"If you have even a shred of doubt about whether we are going to win this game," he told them, "then get off this bus right now."

The world had plenty of doubt, built on the version of Carolina it had watched face Duke on February 5, when the Tar Heels perhaps overthought how they wanted to match up against the Blue Devils. Bacot earned two quick fouls attempting to guard Paolo Banchero. He sat for just over five minutes, and by the time he reentered the game, Duke led, 27–8. From there the game was never in dispute.

This time, it was going to be different.

"That was my fault," Hubert Davis said of the first meeting. "I spent too much time trying to figure out how we were going to defend them. The second game, I just explained how we were going to score, and then I told them they had to figure out how to guard their defensive assignment. We just had to play.

"I also told them the only way we could win a game like this was to have a competitive fight. There has to be a physical willingness to get in a fight. We're not going to start one, but we're going to be willing to go there if it's necessary. We talked very little technical basketball during the week. I went down the line and told them we weren't going to mix any matchups. I told Brady he had Paolo, and either he can guard him or Paolo is going to get 30 on him. I told RJ he had to guard Wendell Moore or Trevor Keels, and if he let them post him up, then he was going to get embarrassed on national television. I wasn't going to take him out. I made it very clear to our team that it was up to them to fight back, to do anything they could to compete."

"That's a challenge you want as a player," RJ Davis said. "You want to play in the bright lights and on the big stage. It didn't bother me, because that's how it is in New York. You always have a good point guard matchup, because there are always great guards in New York. There's no running from it. Plant your feet and guard your man. That's nothing new to me."

Brady Manek made five three-pointers and scored 20 points to go with 11 rebounds and three assists at Duke.

PHOTO BY MAGGIE HOBSON

Caleb Love scored 22 points in Durham, his second straight 20-point game at Duke.

PHOTO BY MAGGIE HOBSON

Hubert Davis showed the Tar Heels plenty of tape in the week before the game. But it was very rarely game tape from the first meeting. Instead, it was tape from other physical, competitive, intense rivalry games. The Tar Heels watched a clip from a documentary on the Lakers-Celtics rivalry. They saw footage from previous Carolina-Duke games such as the bloody Montross battle and Tyler Hansbrough taking a forearm from Gerald Henderson in the face.

"I'm not saying this is what's going to happen in this game," Davis told his team. "I'm not saying go out and start something. But if something happens, this is how it's going to happen."

Roy Williams frequently said the greatest weapon a coach could possess was a talented team that could be persuaded that no one believed in them. In the first meeting, Davis had a talented team that didn't quite believe in itself. But by the tip-off of the second meeting, the belief had arrived.

"It was great having everyone against us," RJ Davis said. "There are always going to be people who have a lot to say who don't really know what this team is about. To be part of the small group and the inner circle that all believed in each other and in this team, we knew we were going to be part of history. It's the greatest feeling in the world."

"At that point, we knew what we had," Bacot said. "We were ready to throw the first punch from the jump."

The game also showcased the evolution of Hubert Davis as a coach over the course of his first year. In the first meeting, Bacot's early foul trouble was decisive. In the second, Bacot was whistled for a foul just 2:58 into the game. Davis immediately subbed him out in favor of Puff Johnson. The Tar Heels could survive Bacot picking up one foul at a time; they couldn't live with him getting two quick fouls in a short stretch, as he often had throughout his Carolina career. So Davis eliminated that possibility and eventually got 30 minutes of playing time from his center, who shot 10 for 11 from the field on the way to scoring 23 points, finishing with just two fouls.

The legend of the Iron Five was born in the typical sweltering heat of Cameron Indoor Stadium. By the second media time-out of the game, RJ Davis had already noticed the unusual heat and asked athletic trainer Doug Halverson to provide him with a cool towel during breaks. But the starters played the entire second half.

They were still fresh enough to lead for the final 9:16 of action, including a pair of huge three-pointers from Brady Manek, and stretch it to double figures by the game's closing minute. The expected Duke run never materialized, leaving a stunned Cameron crowd that included nearly 100 Blue Devil basketball lettermen who wore commemorative Krzyzewski T-shirts for what was supposed to be a celebration.

"We kept getting stops," said RJ Davis. "Coach Davis has a drill where we have to go stop-stop-stop in practice. We've been in these situations where we have to get the stops while we're scoring at the other end. We were prepared for that situation. Once it hit the two-minute mark, and we had that long stretch of stops and scores, I knew the game was under wraps."

While the sellout crowd, many of whom had paid thousands of dollars for tickets, sat mostly quietly in their Cameron Indoor Stadium seats awaiting the postgame speeches and ceremony honoring Krzyzewski, the Tar Heels celebrated steps away from the court in the tiny visitor's locker room.

The Tar Heels celebrated at Duke then headed to Chapel Hill to join the celebration on Franklin Street.
PHOTO BY MAGGIE HOBSON

Hubert Davis wrapped each of the five in a hug. "I'm so proud of you," he told them as each player—and their head coach—fought back tears.

There was one person who was not part of the celebration but who the Tar Heel players wanted to ensure felt included. Bacot had tried to persuade Roy Williams to attend the game, but the retired coach refused, feeling he would be a distraction. So as the players celebrated in the locker room, Bacot FaceTimed his former coach.

"He was a part of this success," Bacot said. "It wasn't all about us. He helped put together this team, and he gave us the opportunity to play for Coach Davis. He believed in us, and he believed in Coach Davis and made sure we would have that next great coach to play for.

"We also knew he didn't get a retirement tour, because he isn't that type of person. We called him because we knew he would be excited, and we wanted to see his reaction. Not many people outside of the players and coaches believed in us, but he did. It was a special moment." •

Caleb Love was one of five starters to play all 20 minutes in the second half at Duke, leading to the nickname the Iron Five.

PHOTO BY MAGGIE HOBSON

Armando Bacot's dunk with 52 seconds to play gave UNC a 10-point lead.

PHOTO BY HELEN MCGINNIS / *DAILY TAR HEEL*

Carolina fans were excited to send the team to New Orleans for the 2022 Final Four.
PHOTO BY MAGGIE HOBSON

Experiences

For all the celebration that followed the victory over Duke, the most significant moments may have come away from Cameron. Davis knew exactly how he wanted his team to celebrate and was ready to leave almost as soon as the final buzzer sounded. In fact, he had to be reminded that his team still had to fulfill postgame media responsibilities before they could hop back on the bus.

After the Tar Heels did every interview, including visits for Davis and Brady Manek to the ACC Network set outside Cameron, finally it was time to load up. But the destination was not the Smith Center, where the team usually returned after a road win. Instead, Davis announced, "We're going to Franklin Street."

This plan had been greeted with skepticism by some members of his staff, who wondered if the impossible-to-miss vehicle, newly wrapped in Carolina graphics with a giant Jumpman logo on the back, would be able to navigate the near mob scene in the celebratory heart of town.

"Take the bus there," Davis said simply.

The ride to Franklin Street was predictably rowdy. Players cranked music, with Davis's new favorite, Lil Durk, getting heavy airplay. This time, there were no clean versions. Davis wasn't singing along with all the words, but he wasn't frowning, either. This was too much fun. "Turn it up!" he told his team.

Those on board were already receiving texts and videos from friends on Franklin and from fans on Twitter and Instagram tagging them. Sometimes, the second Duke matchup falls during spring break, meaning campus is relatively empty even after a win. This time, though, spring break was still a week away. Fraternities, restaurants, and bars had been packed for the game, and as soon as it was over, everyone had only one thought: get to Franklin Street.

Hubert Davis joined his college coach Bill Guthridge as first-year head coaches to lead their teams to the Final Four.
PHOTO BY MAGGIE HOBSON

Carolina fans welcomed home the team after the win over Saint Peter's in Philadelphia sent UNC to its 21st Final Four.

Seeing the videos on their phones was one way to experience it. But seeing it in person, as the bus crawled up to the middle of town, was completely different.

"It's so surreal," said RJ Davis. "Seeing all those people rushing Franklin is one thing. To know that we were the cause of them rushing Franklin, that's an amazing moment. I get goose bumps thinking about it. It puts a smile on your face for the rest of the night, and it really makes you realize that you made history. It was the biggest rivalry in basketball, something you always dream about being part of. To share that moment with not just my teammates but all the students, those are memories we will have forever.

"That's the first time I think I really understood Carolina basketball. Being a part of that history and having that experience, that was my moment for sure."

It was just the moment the team's head coach was chasing. Returning players on the 2022 roster had experienced only a shadow of Carolina basketball for two seasons. The 2020 team was limited by injury and would have missed the NCAA Tournament—before the entire event was canceled because of the pandemic. The 2021 squad mostly played in an empty Smith Center, had to be tested for COVID on a twice-weekly basis, and participated in a pared-down version of the NCAA Tournament. With little of the usual pageantry, the Tar Heels stayed in Indianapolis, were bused to the site of their opening game in West Lafayette, and went right back home after a loss to Wisconsin.

Student life had been every bit as strange: much of the campus took classes online and lived out routines in masks and protective bubbles. Members of the sophomore class were sitting in the locker room over the summer when a manager mentioned the Bell Tower, one of the iconic structures on campus. "What's that?" Kerwin Walton asked. He'd never had the experience of walking across campus and hearing the bells chime the hour. When he heard about the discussion, Davis instantly began making plans to have a manager take the sophomores on a campus tour, almost as if they were brand-new freshmen—which in some ways, they were.

Perhaps the most momentous victory of the 2021 season came in a 91–87 win at Cameron. Caleb Love scored 25 points, six Tar Heels scored in double figures, and Leaky Black hit two clutch free throws to put the game away. It was the type of victory in college basketball's best rivalry that deserved to be celebrated. But the most lasting memory from the game was the fact that a handful of Tar Heel players attended a postgame party and were filmed without masks. The recording spread online immediately, and the season's next opponent, Miami, declined to play the game, citing "safety reasons."

In 2022, with signs the pandemic was easing and campus life steadily returning to something more normal, Davis wanted his team to get the complete post-Duke celebration experience. His team was still new to some of the perks of being a Carolina basketball player. So he gave the players very simple instructions as the bus approached Franklin Street: "When the bus got there, I told the guys, 'If you want to stay down here, do it. I'll take your bags into the Smith Center and put them in your locker. You have to experience this.' They were just floored at what was going on."

The players declined to allow their coaching staff to unload the bus alone. But once they put all their bags inside and changed clothes, almost everyone went back to Franklin Street, where they celebrated safely and without incident, just as generations of Tar Heel players had done before them. It was a signature night not just for the team but for the entire university, the kind of evening that reminded everyone that part of the uniqueness of Carolina basketball has always been that the program is part of the town and community, not above it.

Rob Landry, Jackson Watkins, Ryan McAdoo, Duwe Farris, and Creighton Lebo celebrate the Final Four berth.

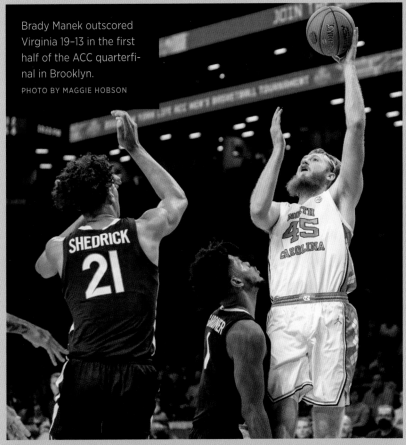

Brady Manek outscored Virginia 19–13 in the first half of the ACC quarterfinal in Brooklyn.
PHOTO BY MAGGIE HOBSON

Carolina's six-game winning streak came to an end against Virginia Tech in the ACC semifinals.
PHOTO BY MAGGIE HOBSON

UNC · 63
Virginia · 43
MARCH 10, 2022

Virginia Tech · 72
UNC · 59
MARCH 11, 2022

The Tar Heels entered the ACC Tournament in Brooklyn on a roll, riding a five-game winning streak.

Led largely by Brady Manek, UNC grinded out a 63–43 win over Virginia in the quarterfinal. The Cavaliers' 43 points were the fewest allowed by Carolina in an ACC Tournament game since 1982 and the fewest in any ACC Tournament game in the shot clock era (which began in 1985–86).

Manek outscored Virginia by himself, 19–13, in the first half and finished the game with 21. It was his third consecutive game scoring 20 or more and part of a hot streak he would continue through the NCAA Tournament.

Armando Bacot had 10 points and 11 rebounds for his 24th double-double, setting a new UNC single-season record. RJ Davis had a then career-high eight rebounds as Carolina won at least one game in the ACC Tournament for an eighth consecutive year.

The Tar Heels' winning streak ended in the ACC semifinals against eventual champion Virginia Tech. UNC came into the game averaging over eight made three-pointers per game and shooting 37.1 percent from behind the stripe, but the Tar Heels went three for 26 (11.5 percent) against the Hokies.

With 19 points and 14 rebounds, Bacot was the lone bright spot in a 72–59 defeat.

Carolina shot under 40 percent from the floor in all four halves in Brooklyn, hitting just nine of 49 three-point tries (18.4 percent). As a result, UNC's ACC Tournament run ended in the semifinal round for the third consecutive year.

UNC · 95
Marquette · 63

MARCH 17, 2022

Brady Manek scored a season-high 28 points in the 32-point win over Marquette in Fort Worth.

PHOTO BY MAGGIE HOBSON

Carolina entered its first NCAA Tournament game in Fort Worth, Texas, as a no. 8 seed, tying for the lowest seed in program history.

On the one hand, the Tar Heels had every reason to feel confident, having won 12 of 15 games over the previous two months, including their best effort of the season in the win at Duke less than two weeks earlier. On the other hand, UNC had also been a no. 8 seed in 2021 and was dominated by Wisconsin in a 23-point loss. And this year's no. 9 seed opponent, Marquette, had beaten Carolina, 83–70, in the Smith Center a season earlier, albeit with a very different team and coaching staff.

In Hubert Davis's first NCAA Tournament game as a head coach, the Tar Heels eliminated all doubt early, crushing the Golden Eagles, 95–63. Carolina's 32-point win was the largest margin in an 8–9 game in NCAA Tournament history.

Carolina built a 28-point halftime lead (the second biggest in an NCAA Tournament game in school history) at 53–25, despite shooting 39 percent from the floor. When the Tar Heels then shot 54.5 percent in the second half there was no way Marquette could come close to overcoming the deficit.

Caleb Love scored 21 of his 23 points in the first half, including tying the school NCAA Tournament record with six three-pointers in just the first half alone. Carolina connected on 13 threes, its highest total ever in an NCAA Tournament game, and had assists on a remarkable 29 of 34 baskets. The 29 assists were a season high.

Brady Manek scored a season-high 28 points, posting his fourth 20-point effort in five games. He hit 10 of 15 shots and led all players with 11 rebounds in his fourth double-double as a Tar Heel. RJ Davis dished out a career-high 12 assists with just a single turnover. The 12 assists were the most by a UNC player all season, the most by any Tar Heel since 2012, and the second-most ever in an NCAA Tournament game by a Carolina player.

It was Carolina's first NCAA Tournament win in three years.

From his first day as head coach, Davis had talked about giving the players the same experiences he received as a player. That's part of why he wanted a staff full of Tar Heels. Jeff Lebo knew the atmosphere in the 1989 ACC Tournament final win over Duke, one of the most intense games in the history of the rivalry. Brad Frederick was part of the 1997 and 1998 Final Four teams. Sean May remembers the fans packing the team hotel at the Adam's Mark in St. Louis after the 2005 national title and greeting the Tar Heels when they returned to Chapel Hill as champions. Although the specific details of those wins might fade, the feelings from the celebrations never go away. Those are the memories Davis wanted to make sure his team made.

The next month was a whirlwind of Tar Heel basketball love. Campus was completely engulfed in following every moment of the Carolina journey through the NCAA Tournament.

The week before the Heels left for New Orleans for the Final Four, Eric Hoots took Manek on the program's golf cart from the Smith Center to Franklin Street for lunch. The reception was as if the president were riding across town. Even Hoots, who has been inside the program for two decades, was rejuvenated by the reception Manek received. And Manek, who played four years at Oklahoma and barely made a ripple, was astonished.

Duwe Farris sported his cowboy hat the players bought in Fort Worth during the first week of the NCAA Tournament.

PHOTO BY MAGGIE HOBSON

"I had first noticed how different things are at Carolina for the basketball players at the football games," Manek said. "The recognition they get just by being in the stands is amazing to me. And slowly, throughout the year, it increased, and even though I was the new guy, people still treated me that same way. I had never played a game for Carolina a few months ago. And by the time we got to the Final Four, just going across campus for lunch, it was incredible how many people knew my name or shouted, 'Go Heels!' or wanted a picture or an autograph. You can't understand it unless you've lived through it."

Davis wanted to maximize the ability for his players to have such moments. The first time the team loaded the bus at the airport after returning from a successful opening weekend, players asked, "Do you think anybody is going to be at the Smith Center?" Davis just chuckled. He knew.

He also knew the impact it would have on his players to participate in the Final Four, especially in New Orleans. Players were given some leeway to take in the scene on Bourbon Street. Team dinners took place in the heart of town, among the growing throng that was assembling for the games. And when Carolina visited the cavernous Superdome for the first time on Thursday, Davis knew exactly how he wanted to treat that moment.

"I really just wanted them to enjoy the experience," he recalled. "I told them all to get their phones so we could go out to the court [and] they could record everything. It was great for them to all have their own pictures and videos of seeing how big everything was. They enjoyed being with each other. They enjoyed going on this ride together."

In 2022, most players try to maintain an air of having seen everything before. But even they were awed by the Superdome. Love, who had already been amazed at the intangible status confirmation of a rapidly ballooning Instagram follower count, looked around at the 70,602 seats. "All of these are going to be filled for the game?" he asked. Told they would be, he gawked.

Hubert Davis encouraged his team to soak in the moment as they walked onto the Superdome court for the first time for practice on Thursday of Final Four weekend.
PHOTO BY MAGGIE HOBSON

"Coach Davis always tells us he wants to experience the things he experienced," RJ Davis said. "He wanted us to capture the moment and have memories to look back on. Having our phones out, we realized we're really in the Final Four in the Superdome in New Orleans. Us being around each other and having fun in practice, practicing in front of 25,000 people at the open practice, getting a feel for the actual court—all of that helped us. We had dealt with our nerves already, so we were able to be loose on the court. When you're having fun, you're going to be better than if you're so serious all the time."

How big was the setting in New Orleans? Even Hubert Davis had an experience that made a big impression. At Friday's open practice, veteran Villanova coach Jay Wright—who was days away from retiring, although no one knew it—pulled Davis aside. "I'm proud of you," Wright told Davis. "And I just want you to know, you can't get to the Final Four by being lucky. You have to be good."

That's the type of month it was for Carolina basketball. Even a veteran coach who had played at every level of the game had experiences that made a big impression on him. And if that's the case for a basketball lifer, imagine the impact it had on the players.

"That's a big part of why I think all the guys are coming back," Hubert Davis said after the season. "They've enjoyed being on that stage. They heard us talking about it and they finally got there. They worked so hard to get there, they got a taste of it, and then they're just going to leave? No. They want to experience it a little more. The emotions they felt after the game in Durham, they were like, 'I finally see what these coaches were talking about. That's why you guys keep telling us about this.' And they wanted to keep being part of that."

Love is one of those who is coming back for another season in Chapel Hill. His reasoning is very simple. "I had one of the best years of my life," he said. "I'm so grateful for all the experiences I had. This year, I really feel like I got the full Carolina experience. The guys on this team are always going to have a special place in my heart. I wouldn't choose anyone else to have done all of this with." •

Carolina's starters with Turner/CBS for the Final Four broadcast.
PHOTO BY MAGGIE HOBSON

Carolina won 15 of 19 games when RJ Davis scored 15 or more points.

New Opportunities

The full student-athlete experience of the 2022 season was very different from what Hubert Davis and the other members of the Carolina coaching staff remembered from their college days.

In the summer of 2021, the NCAA had opened up possibilities for college athletes to profit off of their name, image, and likeness (NIL). With very little guidance, no one was certain what would happen next. As the Tar Heels became more successful in February and March, more opportunities presented themselves for the Carolina players.

Most dabbled in name, image, and likeness deals, joining the personalized electronic greeting service Cameo or working with designers to create unique player-based T-shirts. RJ Davis was one of the Tar Heels with his own shirt, as he commissioned a design based on him flashing the "three goggles" celebration after a made three-pointer.

Davis was fortunate that his parents were willing to handle most of his business transactions. Robert and Venessa Davis were instrumental in his basketball career while he was growing up but also played a much bigger role. For example, Davis is one of the very few Tar Heels who, when given a choice about making an appointment, might voluntarily select nine thirty in the morning, an unheard-of time for a college student. Even more surprisingly, Davis will then invariably show up five minutes early for the appointment.

"That comes from my mom," he said. "At a young age, she always made sure I was on time. And my dad would always leave really early to get us to basketball games. They instilled it in me at a very young age. I was late to a basketball game in the fifth grade at Rucker Park. I got there at halftime. I knew then that I never wanted to be late again."

Davis's parents taught him the value of timing in a variety of ways. By early March, Davis had a new batch of shirts with his image ready to sell. But his parents advised him to wait for the right moment, to capitalize on a big game and then release it. That game happened when Carolina took down defending national champion Baylor in Fort Worth in the second round of the NCAA Tournament.

RJ Davis led Carolina in assists and was second in three-point and free throw percentages.

PHOTO BY JEFFREY A. CAMARATI

UNC · 93
Baylor · 86 (OT)

It was, by any measure, one of the most ridiculous, entertaining, heart-stopping, jaw-dropping basketball games Carolina has ever played. It just happened to come in the second round of the NCAA Tournament against the top seed in the East Region and the defending national champion.

That Carolina upset Baylor, 93–86, in overtime is fact. How it happened was almost too bizarre to be believed.

Twice before, Carolina had eliminated a no. 1 seed in the second round: first as a no. 8 seed in 1990 when Rick Fox banked in the game-winner as time expired to send Billy Tubbs and his no. 1-ranked Oklahoma Sooners packing in Austin, Texas, and a decade later, also as a no. 8 seed, when Joseph Forte and Julius Peppers helped lead UNC past Stanford in Birmingham, Alabama.

The game was in Fort Worth, Texas, at the palatial Dickies Arena, just 90 minutes from Baylor's campus in Waco.

UNC started slowly as the Bears' Adam Flagler hit an elbow jumper 14 seconds into the game and Kendall Brown stole a lazy cross-court pass and laid it in for a 4–0 Baylor lead. Carolina didn't crack the scoreboard until more than two minutes into the contest. But RJ Davis hit a pair of threes and eight straight points to give the Tar Heels the lead.

Carolina would hold that lead for the next 37:06. For nearly 23 and a half minutes, the Tar Heels led by double figures, including a nearly three-and-a-half-minute stretch midway through the second half when the advantage was 20 or more points.

Davis hit four of his five threes and scored 17 of his career-best 30 in the first half as the Tar Heels shot 50 percent from

The overtime win over Baylor marked the first time Carolina ever eliminated the defending champion in the NCAA Tournament.

PHOTO BY MAGGIE HOBSON

the floor and held the Bears to just 40 percent. Carolina had 12 assists on 14 field goals and committed only five turnovers, three fewer than the Bears, against Baylor's relentless defensive pressure.

The first nine minutes and 52 seconds of the second half were all Carolina. Brady Manek scored 17 points and Davis added another 10 as Carolina pushed its lead to 25 with 10:47 to play. Manek made five second-half field goals and was on his way to a career scoring high, but was called for a flagrant two foul while boxing out on a rebound and was ejected with 10:08 to play. The Tar Heels led, 67–45, at the time.

Over the next 10 minutes and eight seconds the Bears outscored the Tar Heels, 35–13, to force overtime.

Caleb Love fouled out with 6:15 remaining, and Armando Bacot drew his fourth foul, momentarily sending him to the sideline at the 4:45 mark.

Playing with reserves Puff Johnson, Justin McKoy, and Dontrez Styles, Carolina increased its lead to nine with 2:37 to go. Turnovers, missed free throws, and hot Baylor shooting, including a banked three-pointer by Jeremy Sochan with 28 seconds left, pulled the Bears to within three at 80–77.

Bacot missed two free throws, and James Akinjo capped the comeback with a three-point play to tie the game with 16 seconds to play in regulation. Carolina had turned the ball over nine times in the final 10 minutes.

Bacot, Leaky Black, Davis, McKoy, and Styles played the entire overtime. Styles, who would play a season-high 25 minutes and score a season-best nine points, improbably opened the scoring with just his third three-pointer of the season. Black scored inside, and Davis converted a left-handed scoop shot for a four-point lead with 78 seconds left to effectively clinch the upset win.

The Bears had made 10 of their final 20 field goal attempts to end regulation, but Carolina held them to one of 11 in overtime.

RJ Davis became the first Tar Heel ever to record double-figure assists in one NCAA game (12 versus Marquette) and 30 points in the next. Manek scored 26 points and was plus-26 while on the floor, 10 better than any other player in the game and 16 better than any other Tar Heel.

The win was the ninth for UNC over a no. 1 seed, which equaled Duke for the most in NCAA Tournament history.

The Tar Heels had easily dispatched Marquette in the first round, cruising through a physical matchup with the Golden Eagles. Davis shot a miserable one for 10 that game, but he also distributed 12 assists and had just one turnover. True to a New York product whose confidence is an important part of his game, the shooting struggles didn't bother him.

"I talked to Jackie Manuel," Davis said. "He told me to be calm, find my rhythm, and I'd be good. That's always how I have been. You're not going to find a rhythm by not shooting the ball. Most of the time, I have no idea how many misses I have. I don't care about how many points I have. It's about winning the game and being confident with every shot you take. Once I hit my first one, I was in that rhythm. I felt loose, and I knew I was taking the next one as soon as I had it."

Davis missed his first one against Baylor but then quickly swished two early three-pointers, celebrating with that same three goggles celebration that would soon launch a very popular shirt. He had eight points in the first 3:29 and 17 points in the first half, and finished with 30.

In the end, the Tar Heels would need every one. After Carolina ran out to a lead that reached as much as 25 points in the second half, Baylor responded aggressively on both ends of the court. Bears forward Jeremy Sochan, who played an instigating style reminiscent of Dennis Rodman—with hair to fit the profile—fell on the floor 17 times in the game, as he always seemed to be involved in some type of contact. At the 12-minute mark, Sochan was whistled for a foul for bulling through the back of Brady Manek while ostensibly trying to earn rebounding position.

"He was constantly chirping," Manek said, "constantly getting into little things with everybody. He's the kind of guy who always has something to say when the other team is at the free throw line—'Give me a miss here,' that kind of stuff—and his team followed his lead, because they all had something to say the entire game. We were killing them, and they were still trying to talk, and we just kept killing them.

"There were a lot of things that went missed in that game. There were a lot of cheap shots and pushing."

The shot that got the most attention, though, was Manek's elbow to Sochan's face with 10:08 remaining. On that same play, Sochan had initiated the contact by pushing Manek in the back while battling for rebounding position. Manek responded.

"Those small things they were doing slowly built into a big thing," Manek said. "I did hit him in the face. I didn't purposely try to hit him,

RJ Davis had a dozen assists versus Marquette, the second most by a Tar Heel in an NCAA Tournament game.

because if I had, he would have known it. But I definitely was trying to make contact with him, because that's how the game was being played."

After one of the nine official reviews during the game, Manek was ejected for a flagrant foul and was escorted to the locker room by Eric Hoots, leaving the two to watch the game on a locker room television that received only a feed of the in-arena video board, not the live game broadcast. It was a painful way to experience Carolina's quickly deteriorating fortunes on the court.

"I genuinely think we were going to blow them out by 40 with Brady," said Leaky Black. "The Biscuit Boys were going to be in there. But when Brady went out, it changed drastically."

In the locker room, Manek asked Hoots to call an Atlantic Coast Conference officiating administrator to confirm he would be eligible to play in the next game if the Tar Heels advanced. The answer was quick: because the play was not ruled a fight, Manek would indeed be eligible in the Sweet 16.

But without the benefit of that information, the players on the court believed Manek would be out not just for the remainder of the Baylor game but for what would eventually be an impending matchup with UCLA. In an on-court huddle shortly after the ejection, Black was trying to provide some instructions on how to handle Baylor's full-court press. But Armando Bacot was, in Black's words, "freaking out."

"I grabbed his chest to try and calm him down," Black said. "But he was like, 'Brady can't play in the next game.' That stopped me real quick. I was like, 'Oh no. He can't play in the next game?' We immediately stopped thinking about Baylor."

The defending national champions immediately took advantage of the Tar Heels' wavering attention. Playing in front of a partisan crowd, they trimmed nine points off the lead in less than a minute. Caleb Love fouled out four minutes after Manek's ejection, and the rattled Tar Heels didn't handle the pressure well, struggling to inbound the ball and to execute their press-breaking set.

"It felt," Black said, "like the clock wasn't running at all."

The Tar Heels had the last shot of regulation, but RJ Davis's long jumper was errant. In the building, it felt like Baylor had all the momentum going into overtime. Surely they would carry their second-half run through the extra period.

But just before tip-off of overtime, RJ Davis gathered the five Tar Heels on the court. "Calm down," he told them. "This is March Madness. It's supposed to be like this. Let's pull this thing through. Play together, and take it possession by possession. We have talent on the floor."

The timely message from one of their leaders settled the Tar Heels. It also opened the door for one of Hubert Davis's season-long messages to be proven correct.

Even when the head coach had shortened his rotation, playing predominantly five players, he had continued to tell the Carolina reserves that they would eventually get an opportunity. "I don't know when that opportunity will come," he told them, "but it will come."

As it turned out, it came in Fort Worth. Dontrez Styles had already played good minutes in the first half, including an extremely difficult finish through contact near the halftime buzzer for a basket. His biggest shot of the day, however, came on the first possession of overtime, when he confidently drilled a corner three-pointer to restore the Tar Heel lead.

"They didn't believe me when I told them the opportunity was coming," Hubert Davis said. "Ask Dontrez and he'll tell you he didn't believe me. He said, 'How do you know it's coming?' And I just told him, 'We say stuff to you because we've actually experienced and been through it. I've been there before in the NBA Playoffs. The week before I wasn't playing, and then I was playing in the playoffs. So I knew this would happen.' But it was one of those things where you can talk to the guys, but until it actually

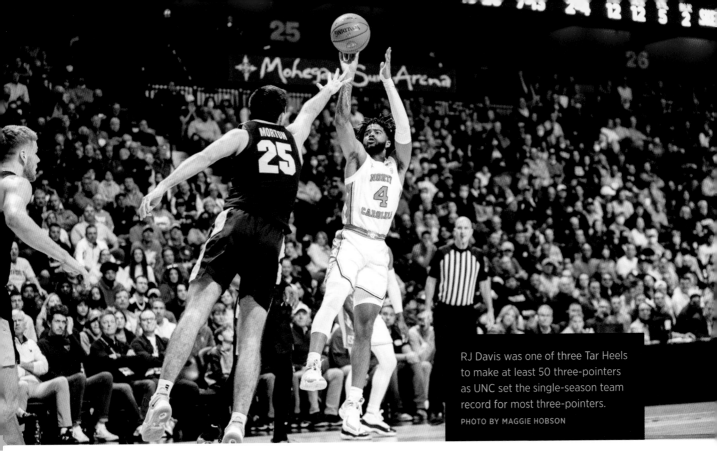

RJ Davis was one of three Tar Heels to make at least 50 three-pointers as UNC set the single-season team record for most three-pointers.
PHOTO BY MAGGIE HOBSON

happens, that's when they really believe you. And from that moment on, they realize they really do have to be ready, because they will be in those situations."

Styles made the shot that restored Carolina's confidence, but it was RJ Davis who finally broke Baylor. With under 90 seconds to play, Davis converted an amazing, driving shot with his left hand and drew a foul. The free throw gave the Tar Heels a six-point lead in a game Carolina eventually won by seven.

It was a quintessential RJ Davis game. Against an opponent no one expected Carolina to beat, facing incredible adversity, the Tar Heels somehow figured out a way to win, largely due to the smallest player in the rotation, who couldn't be stopped.

"I've dealt with adversity my whole life," RJ Davis said. "I've dealt with doubt. I've always felt like people take my game for granted. That instills fire in me. And when I get the chance to try and prove someone wrong, or to help my team in a big situation, that's what I love to do."

His success in the big situation meant the timing was finally right. The new RJ Davis T-shirts went on sale immediately after the game. •

Caleb Love scored 27 of his 30 points in the second half versus UCLA after changing from black to blue shoes at halftime.

PHOTO BY MAGGIE HOBSON

UNC · 73
UCLA · 66

MARCH 25, 2022

Eighth-seeded Carolina faced fourth-seeded UCLA in Philadelphia in the Sweet 16. These two teams had been scheduled to meet in Las Vegas earlier in the season in December, but COVID issues resulted in UNC playing Kentucky there instead.

The Bruins were the favorite, having advanced to the Pac-12 Tournament final the week before and boasting a 27-7 record. The Tar Heels proved to be the better team, however, winning, 73-66, for their sixth consecutive victory versus UCLA and their 17th in a row against Pac-12 opponents.

Caleb Love and Brady Manek each hit three-pointers for UNC's first two baskets in the first 82 seconds of the game, but the game was close for much of the first half. The Bruins built an eight-point lead with 8:33 to go before halftime, but

back-to-back three-pointers by Manek and RJ Davis cut it to two, and UCLA led by three at the break.

Carolina hit six second-half three-pointers, and Love finished with a game-high and career-high 30 points in the best performance of his career. He scored 27 of his 30 points in the second half, hitting six of 13 three-pointers to tie the school NCAA Tournament three-point record for the second time in two weekends (having also hit six threes against Marquette in the first round in Fort Worth).

Love hit a three to take the lead at 67-64 with 1:03 to play (one of 14 lead changes in the back-and-forth battle) and later hit two free throws with 7.8 seconds left to put Carolina ahead by five at 71-66. UNC led for only 8:20 of the game's 40 minutes, by far the least

amount of time in any win all season (the second-least was 15:08 in an overtime game versus Syracuse).

The Tar Heels finished the game on a 12-2 run and continued to show prowess in managing and converting late-game situations into wins. Carolina dominated the boards, including getting 15 on the offensive end, and hit 10 of 31 three-pointers as a team, making it three NCAA Tournament games in a row with 10 or more for the first time in program history.

Armando Bacot had 14 points and 15 rebounds for his 28th double-double of the year and third in a row in the NCAA tourney. With 1:40 remaining, he made one of the key plays of the NCAA Tournament for the Tar Heels, saving a ball from going out of bounds to Love, whose three tied the game at 64 instead of giving the ball back to UCLA.

"That was the turning point of the game," UCLA head coach Mick Cronin said afterward. "We get that rebound, it's different. But you never know what happens. Obviously that's going to keep me up at night."

Manek scored 13 points and grabbed eight rebounds while hitting three three-pointers. He hit a big three-pointer with 4:30 to play. Davis had 12 points and seven rebounds, hitting all five of his free throw tries, including two in the final seconds to ice the win.

With its 15th win in 18 contests, UNC won its 129th all-time NCAA Tournament game, tying Kentucky for the most in history.

Carolina's Sweet 16 win over no. 4 seed UCLA was its 17th straight win over a Pac-12 opponent.

PHOTO BY MAGGIE HOBSON

Caleb Love scored 113 points in six NCAA Tournament games, which tied Brady Manek for the tournament lead by all players in the 68-team field.

PHOTO BY MAGGIE HOBSON

UNC · 69
Saint Peter's · 49

MARCH 27, 2022

After the emotional roller coaster of the UCLA game two days earlier, Carolina entered the NCAA East Region final against Saint Peter's as a decided favorite for the first time in the tournament.

The 15th-seeded Peacocks had upset no. 2 seed Kentucky in the first round and ridden a wave of solid play and momentum to be just one win away from the Final Four in what could have been the most unlikely Cinderella story in NCAA Tournament history.

But like much of the ACC and the nation over the course of the 2021–22 season, Saint Peter's had no answer for Tar Heel Armando Bacot in a 69–49 Carolina win. The big man from Richmond earned Most Outstanding Player honors for the East Region after putting up a dominant 20-point, 22-rebound performance against the Peacocks, his fourth consecutive double-double in NCAA Tournament play.

Bacot's size hindered the Saint Peter's offense and helped limit it to 30 percent shooting from the floor, the lowest by a Tar Heel opponent since the UNC Asheville game in November. Carolina jumped out to a 7–0 lead in the opening three minutes; later led, 21–7, as the Peacocks missed 16 of their first 19 shots; and never trailed. Saint Peter's saw its 10-game winning streak come to an end.

Bacot's 22 rebounds tied the UNC record for most rebounds in an NCAA Tournament game, and with his 29th double-double, he tied Tim Duncan for the most in a season in ACC history. He also moved into fifth place in ACC single-season rebounding, with the most rebounds by any conference player in the past 60 years.

Brady Manek hit seven of 11 shots, including four of six three-point tries, and finished with 19 points. Caleb Love scored 14 despite shooting just two of 10 from behind the arc.

The Peacocks' 49 points were the fewest allowed by Carolina in 28 NCAA Tournament regional final games, and the Tar Heels improved to 21–7 in regional finals.

The win was Carolina's 130th in the NCAA Tournament, breaking a tie with Kentucky for most in the sport's history. It earned the Tar Heels their 21st trip to the Final Four, again the most of any team in NCAA annals. And Carolina moved on to the Final Four for the ninth consecutive decade, something no other program can boast of.

Hubert Davis became one of 10 first-year head coaches to lead a team to the Final Four, a list that includes Bill Guthridge (1998), his own assistant coach when Davis was a player at UNC.

Davis's Tar Heels advanced to the Final Four in New Orleans, setting up an epic matchup with Duke in the Final Four. It would be the first-ever NCAA Tournament meeting between the longtime rivals, on the biggest stage and with the highest stakes.

The Tar Heels became
the first team to advance
to the Final Four in nine
consecutive decades.
PHOTO BY MAGGIE HOBSON

Caleb Love scored 22 of his game-high 28 points in the second half in the Final Four win over Duke.
PHOTO BY MAGGIE HOBSON

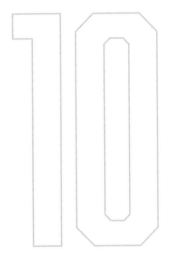

A Classic in the Crescent City

In the days after Carolina dismantled Duke in Mike Krzyzewski's final home game, the Tar Heels noticed that almost all the coverage focused on Duke losing rather than Carolina winning. As they watched ESPN and scanned social media in the days before the rematch in the Final Four, they saw that virtually everyone was picking Duke.

Just before the game, as the Tar Heels prepared to leave their locker room—located directly across the hall from their opponent's—Armando Bacot looked at his teammates. "We've played the best of anybody in this entire tournament," he told them. "And the whole world has no idea what's about to happen to Duke."

The Tar Heels knew. They'd already been energized by one of Hubert Davis's patented pregame speeches, a tactic he learned from Pat Riley. A master motivator, Riley seemed to have a different story for every pregame talk. Davis is similar, and his messages became even more emotional and meaningful as the season progressed.

Before the national semifinal, he walked into a silent Carolina locker room, with the players seated around him. He paced back and forth. He didn't say a word. Then he stopped and looked around the room, with every eye on him.

"You're telling me," he said to his team, "that what's stopping you from getting to the national championship game is *those* dudes?"

"Then he started pacing again," said Leaky Black. "I think he had a tear coming down his cheek. I was ready to play right then. I could have run onto the court at that exact moment. It was like a Denzel Washington speech or something. It gave me chills as soon as he said it. He didn't even have to say much."

"Coach Davis told us if he had it to do over again, and he had Duke in front of him to win a national championship, he would run straight through a brick wall to do it," Caleb Love said. "We had already beaten them once and we knew we could beat them again. They had all the pressure on them. We were still enjoying the moment, and Coach Davis helped take the pressure off us by making sure we enjoyed the moment. New Orleans was a business trip, but we enjoyed it at the same time."

An advantage for the Tar Heels in the third meeting was a new version of Love, who was more comfortable driving to the basket to create offense. He'd struggled occasionally in the postseason, settling too often for perimeter jumpers. Against UCLA, however, he began to get to the basket.

Once he had a little success closer to the rim, he found his outside shot again. The result was an electric 30-point performance against the Bruins in what might have been the most complete 40 minutes of Carolina's tournament run.

Caleb Love was Carolina's second-leading scorer at 15.9 points per game. PHOTO BY JACK MORTON

Caleb Love says Coach Davis sought input from the players, which made them play even harder because he would do a lot for them. PHOTO BY MAGGIE HOBSON

Love has always been a volume scorer, willing to take the next big shot no matter what kind of success he's experienced to that point in the game. But that swagger sometimes overshadows his deep knowledge of the game. He had spent most of his life preparing to play on the game's biggest stage.

"Any time I have downtime, you might think I'm watching Netflix, but I'm probably watching YouTube clips or film on someone," he said. "I always want to be ahead of the next guy. I was never really a party kind of dude. I want to learn the game, whether it's stuff on the court or learning about how some of the great players led their teams. Everyone has a different leadership style. I wanted to make sure I understood how to do things like them."

Caleb Love averaged 17.4 points in Carolina's 29 wins.
PHOTO BY MAGGIE HOBSON

UNC · 81
Duke · 77

APRIL 2, 2022

A longtime columnist for the Raleigh *News and Observer* described it as the "biggest sporting event in the history of North Carolina."

The impact wasn't limited to the Old North State, either. The national semifinal between Carolina and Duke drew the second-highest cable ratings ever for college basketball, even higher than the championship game two nights later. It dominated the airwaves and social media channels from the moment the Tar Heels beat Saint Peter's to win the East Regional and lock in a Final Four berth opposite the Blue Devils, who had advanced to New Orleans the previous evening by defeating Arkansas.

Carolina and Duke played for the 258th time over 103 seasons, but it was the first-ever meeting in an NCAA Tournament game and just the second in any kind of postseason other than a conference tournament.

Amazingly, the teams came to New Orleans having split their previous 106 games, with each winning 53 times and, even more remarkably, having scored 8,261 points apiece in those games.

It was Hubert Davis's 38th game as a head coach, while Duke's Mike Krzyzewski was coaching in his 1,570th overall and his 1,438th with the Blue Devils.

The Superdome hummed with an energy that felt noticeably different from

that of other Final Fours. Seemingly no one left after the Kansas-Villanova game, as fans of those teams and of college basketball in general were ready to watch this greatest of all rivalries play out on the sport's grandest stage.

RJ Davis, who had scored 21 and engineered Carolina's 55-point second half at Duke, kept Carolina within striking distance in the first half with 14 points. Twice the Blue Devils built six-point leads, but both times the Tar Heels responded with 6–0 runs to even the score. Jeremy Roach's three-point play with three seconds to go provided Duke with a 37–34 advantage heading into halftime.

Leaky Black led a UNC defense that held Duke to 40 percent shooting in the second half.
PHOTO BY MAGGIE HOBSON

RJ Davis had 18 points, seven rebounds, and four assists versus Duke in the semifinals.

The Blue Devils scored the first four points of the second half and threatened to pull away at 41–34, but Carolina rocked the Superdome with 13 unanswered points. Caleb Love began the burst with back-to-back threes; Brady Manek gave UNC its first lead in more than 13 minutes with another quick-release bomb; and Love added a pair of driving buckets to put the Tar Heels ahead, 47–41, with 16 minutes to play.

In a game that included a dozen ties and 18 lead changes, 13 of which came in the second half, the Blue Devils would lead again but never by more than two points. Over the final 15:42, the margin for either team exceeded three points—a single possession—for all of 104 seconds.

Carolina would score nine different times in the second half either to break a tie or reverse the lead, including field goals or free throws by all five Tar Heel starters.

Armando Bacot, who finished with 21 rebounds, most in the Final Four in 19 seasons, twice grabbed offensive boards and scored to break ties; Leaky Black nailed a three for a 52–51 lead; and three times Manek buried a three-pointer to put UNC back on top, the third of which gave the Tar Heels a 73–71 lead with 1:41 to play.

Wendell Moore followed Manek with Duke's fifth three of the game for what proved to be the Devils' final lead of the night. RJ Davis gave UNC the lead for

good with a pair of free throws, after which Mark Williams missed two from the stripe with 46 seconds remaining that could have tied the game or given Duke the lead.

On the ensuing possession, Love, who scored 22 of his game-high 28 points in the half, extended UNC's lead to 78–74 with a three just over Williams's outstretched hands with 24.8 seconds to play. It was *the* shot in the game that will be replayed for generations.

Love went on to make three of four free throws over the final 17 seconds to clinch Carolina's 12th national championship game appearance and, arguably, its most memorable win in series history.

His moment to demonstrate what he had learned came in the final minutes of a close national semifinal game. Duke had seized a seven-point lead just a minute into the second half. But Brady Manek ignited a 13–0 run with a terrific sequence that included him blocking Paolo Banchero's shot on an attempted drive. At the start of the game, Manek had been frustrated to see that Banchero intended to face guard him to prevent him from getting open looks. But the veteran Manek also knew that that type of defensive intensity sometimes wanes as fatigue sets in.

After blocking Banchero's shot, Manek—not a speedster—noticed Banchero was somewhat lackadaisical getting back on defense. Manek sprinted down the sideline and ran hard to the opposite corner. Manek's three-pointer gave Carolina a two-point lead and prompted him to roar, "Bang, bang!" (followed by a certain adjective) as he ran back on defense, a celebration that will likely live forever in Tar Heel lore.

"That was the buildup of the whole season against them," Manek said. "When we played them in Chapel Hill, they were beating us really good and chirping at us the whole time. They earned it, and they were letting us have it. But then in the game at Cameron, we were beating them and they were still talking. Caleb was shooting free throws to put us up by double figures, and Trevor Keels looked at me and said, 'Are you guys even going to make the NCAA Tournament?' He said the same thing to Caleb. Those small things built up to that moment. I was just like, 'I'm over these guys.' I didn't like the way they treated the game. And it felt really good to get the lead and get that momentum."

The situation didn't feel quite as good a few minutes later, when Armando Bacot went down after stepping on Black's ankle with 5:18 remaining.

"Initially, it was some of the worst pain I've ever felt in my life," Bacot said.

Brady Manek's lightning-fast trigger gave UNC a 73–71 lead in the Super-dome with less than two minutes to play.

Teammates Ryan McAdoo (left) and Duwe Farris (right) helped Armando Bacot off the floor after he injured his ankle with 5:18 to play against Duke. Trainer Doug Halverson worked with Bacot to get him back in the game after just 42 seconds elapsed off the clock.

PHOTO BY MAGGIE HOBSON

Caleb Love's three-pointer with 24 seconds to play gave the Tar Heels a four-point lead over Duke in the national semifinals and will be remembered as one of the greatest shots in Carolina history.

PHOTO BY RICHARD DEUTSCH / USA TODAY

Caleb Love scored 22 of UNC's 47 second-half points in the national semifinal win over Duke.

PHOTO BY MAGGIE HOBSON

The air went out of the Superdome. Bacot, Carolina's indispensable post presence, had to be helped off the court. He'd first thought he was definitely done for the game. But as he began to move around, he saw the situation differently.

On the Tar Heel sideline, he was evaluated by athletic trainer Doug Halverson, who felt it was a typical ankle sprain, an annoying and painful injury almost every high-level athlete has suffered at some point. Halverson was honest with Bacot.

"There is no magic fix for this," he told the junior. "We had this situation with Joel Berry in 2017. The pain will lessen as you move but it may not go away completely." Halverson told Bacot he had a choice: "Is the pain enough to stop you, or are you able to work through it?"

Bacot began testing his ankle by walking around the Carolina bench, moving under his own power, slowly gaining confidence on his ankle and passing the necessary medical examination. Eventually, he stopped.

Senior Leaky Black celebrates the Final Four win over Duke with his family.
PHOTO BY MAGGIE HOBSON

"That's when I realized that this was the biggest college basketball game of all time," Bacot said. "I knew what was at stake. I'm a Carolina fan, too. The bragging rights to say we beat Duke on that stage meant something to me. I wanted to be part of that story. And if I had to play through a little pain in my ankle to be part of it, I was going to do it."

Less than a minute of game time after leaving the court, Bacot checked back in. He'd left in a tie game, and he returned—thanks to two clutch free throws from Puff Johnson—to find the same situation.

That set the stage for one of the most indelible moments of the Carolina-Duke rivalry. With a one-point Carolina lead, Duke's Mark Williams missed two free throws. Johnson boxed out Wendell Moore to allow Love to snag the rebound with 46 seconds remaining.

"I walked the ball up the court, and I really thought Coach Davis was going to call a time-out," Love said.

"I thought about it," Davis said. "But I felt we were going to get the shot we wanted. I just felt calm."

RJ Davis gave Carolina the lead for good with a pair of free throws with a minute to play.
PHOTO BY MAGGIE HOBSON

Hubert Davis addressed the team in the locker room in New Orleans after the Tar Heels beat Duke, 81–77, to advance to the national championship game. PHOTO BY MAGGIE HOBSON

Carolina's starters, including Armando Bacot, scored 79 of their 81 points against Duke in New Orleans. PHOTO BY MAGGIE HOBSON

Almost no one else in the crowd of 70,062 felt calm. The moment, with the outcome of the biggest game in the history of the sport's best rivalry hanging in the balance, was excruciating.

"Coach Davis trusted me with the ball," Love said. "I saw Leaky had Williams on him. Coach Davis told Leaky to come set a screen, and I knew they would switch. So now I've got Mark Williams on me. I didn't know he was going to back up like he did. If he hedged, I was going to split the middle and go downhill. If he switched up onto me, I was going to back up and do a move to get downhill to create either for myself or someone else. But when I came off the screen and he backed up, I saw a little room. I just rose up and shot it with confidence. I knew it was good when it left my hand."

"I didn't feel like Duke was organized," Hubert Davis said. "But I felt we were organized. I think I would have called a time-out if we were tied or if we were down. But I felt like we knew exactly what we wanted and what we could get. Leaky almost went a little earlier to set the screen, but I told him to wait, and then with about 14 seconds left I told him to go. And I felt really good about Caleb taking that shot. I knew he was going to hit it."

Sitting in the Smith Center locker room recounting the play several weeks after it happened, it seems almost impossible that Love was able to process that many variables under that much stress in that situation. What, exactly, made him decide to elevate for an enormous three-pointer at a time when he'd had better success going to the basket and had missed his last four three-pointers?

It was a combination of studying the game intently . . . and having just the right amount of bravado.

"Knowing Mark, I knew he likes to play that drop coverage," he said. "If he backed up, I could have gone to the basket, but he could have blocked my shot. So I just went for the dagger."

Because the dagger is always the way Caleb Love plays, right? The St. Louis native smiled broadly.

"Facts," he said with a satisfied grin. •

Hall of Fame coach Roy Williams was exuberant watching his former assistant Hubert Davis lead UNC to a Final Four win over Duke.
PHOTO BY ROBERT CRAWFORD

Newlyweds Trent and Sara Myers walked from their wedding reception at the Carolina Inn to Franklin Street to celebrate the Final Four win over Duke.
PHOTO BY KATIE WILSON

TAR HEELS WIN

TAR HEELS WIN

The Tar Heels defeated Duke to advance to the national championship game in the first-ever meeting between the two teams in the NCAA Tournament.

PHOTO BY MAGGIE HOBSON

The Carolina Basketball Family showed out in force in New Orleans to support the Tar Heels in the Final Four. PHOTO BY UNC ATHLETICS

Bacot's 31st double-double tied him with Navy's David Robinson for the all-time NCAA single-season record.

PHOTO BY MAGGIE HOBSON

11

A Community Comes Together

Two nights later, Carolina was locked in a close battle with Kansas for the national championship. Needing a stop in the game's final minutes, the Tar Heels set up in man-to-man defense. And as the Jayhawks brought the ball to the frontcourt, there was Hubert Davis on the Carolina sideline, clapping his hands, an enormous smile on his face.

That type of calmness under pressure and enjoyment of the moment defined the first season of the Hubert Davis era.

"Basketball is fun for me," Davis said. "Other than my wife and kids, that's always been my happy place. It doesn't matter what the scenario is. I'm not stressed, I'm not worried, I'm not nervous. My experience has been that whether what happens in a basketball game is good or bad, something good is going to come of it. I believe that because that's what has happened in my life. So I really am having fun on the sideline.

"Because of losing my mom at a young age, I know things aren't guaranteed. So why would I waste an experience of coaching North Carolina or being in the Final Four? Enjoy the moment and enjoy the experience. You don't know if you're going to have this again. In 1991, after I played in the Final Four, I said, 'I want to play in this again.' I didn't get back as a player. In my second year in the NBA, I was so worried about how many minutes I was playing that I didn't play my best in the [1994] NBA Finals. I told myself I would have a better perspective when I got back to the Finals, and I never made it back again. So I want these guys to enjoy the moment when it is happening."

"When you see your head coach over there clapping and smiling in that type of situation, it makes a difference," said RJ Davis. "It makes it more fun to play for him. He has that energy like he's on the court with you, and you feed off that as a player."

Players still marvel at their coach's demeanor in the final seconds of the win at Clemson. Remember, this is long before the Iron Five, long before the Final Four. This was February 8, just three days after being dismantled by Duke in the Smith Center. Carolina was a relatively pedestrian 16–7 overall and 8–4 in the ACC.

Puff Johnson scored nine of his 11 points in the second half of the national championship game.
PHOTO BY MAGGIE HOBSON

With 15 seconds left in a tie game, Davis called time-out. He gathered his team around him.

"This is awesome!" he said. "If I'd told you when you were a little kid that you'd get to play for North Carolina, and you'd go play on the road at Clemson and get the ball with 15 seconds left in a tie game, you'd just giggle and smile. This is great. Now here's what we're going to do."

It worked, as Caleb Love drove and found Brady Manek for the game-winning basket with 3.1 seconds remaining.

"He's kept the same personality every single day," Manek said. "It was so cool to watch his progress throughout the year. It's his first year as a head coach, and people were getting on him at times, but now he's the hero. He always talked to us about ignoring the noise. That's what he did throughout the year."

Maintaining his approach helped restore Carolina basketball to what Davis always believed was its rightful place among the nation's elite. The in-season chatter about whether Carolina was a "soft" team wasn't disrespectful to just the current squad. Under Davis, they realized it was also an unfair commentary on the program's past.

"Look, we've got coaches on our staff who were coached by Dean Smith and Bill Guthridge," said Armando Bacot. "When you call us soft, it's like calling them soft. It's like calling Michael Jordan soft. We may not be good. We may not be able to shoot. We might play badly in a game. But don't call North Carolina soft. That's never a word that should be associated with this program, and I hope we showed that to people this year."

Prior to this season, no one on the Carolina roster had ever played in a Final Four. Davis helped get them there. He showed them what it took to advance in the NCAA Tournament, how precious the possessions are when you're trying to move into the next round of the postseason. That will matter. With four starters returning for the 2022–23 season, they'll bring back with them the experiences from 2021–22.

"I was standing there with Armando before the national championship game during the national anthem, and I was like, 'Look around, we're really here,'" said Leaky Black. "Making it to the Final Four is the Carolina standard. You can't describe that experience to anyone. You have to walk out on the court and see the 70,000 people for yourself and look in the stands and see how proud your family is."

Kansas · 72
UNC · 69

APRIL 4, 2022

Forty-eight hours after Carolina beat Duke in the ACC rivals' first-ever NCAA Tournament game, the Tar Heels played Kansas for the national championship. It was the fifth time these programs, which are two of the three winningest teams in college basketball history, played each other in the Final Four. No other pair in Final Four history had ever matched up so frequently.

The game wouldn't go to triple overtime like in 1957, when the Tar Heels defeated Wilt Chamberlain's Jayhawks to cap a perfect 32–0 season. But it did come down to the last minute, even to the very final possession.

Kansas was the lone no. 1 seed to make it to New Orleans and defeated Big East champion Villanova in the semifinals.

Carolina spent Sunday and Monday resting and recovering from its 81–77 win over the Blue Devils, with all eyes on Armando Bacot's sprained right ankle.

The Tar Heels went through a short workout Sunday at the Superdome, going over the pregame scout for Kansas and doing some light running and shooting. The team passed on a midday shootaround Monday, opting for additional rest. Bacot stayed off his ankle and received round-the-clock treatments, which would allow him to stay on the court for more than 38 minutes.

The teams played in front of 69,423 fans, and the game developed over roughly four segments, as the two teams took turns as the preeminent force.

Carolina misfired on its initial four shots while Kansas scored the first seven points to lead 9–3 at the first television time-out. Bacot's three-point play gave Carolina its first lead at 12–11, and the game was deadlocked at 22 with six minutes to play in the half.

The Tar Heels then reeled off 16 straight points over the next three and a half minutes to take a 38–22 lead. Brady Manek drilled back-to-back threes to begin the assault, and Bacot and RJ Davis scored five points apiece to hand Kansas its largest deficit of the NCAA Tournament and third-largest of the season.

Puff Johnson's offensive rebound and basket with one second to play in the half sent the teams to the locker rooms with Carolina in front, 40–25. The Tar Heel defense held the Jayhawks to 10 of 33 field goals. Bacot had 12 points and 10 rebounds, becoming the first player in NCAA Tournament history with six double-doubles in a single postseason.

He had four offensive rebounds, which helped UNC build an 18–2 edge in second-chance points.

The second 40 minutes began like the first, with KU scoring six straight points and Carolina missing three shots and committing a pair of turnovers that helped the Jayhawks quickly carve into the 15-point margin.

Caleb Love hit a three and then a two-pointer to keep the lead at 12, before an 8–0 Kansas run made it 45–41 Carolina with 14:15 to play.

Johnson's dunk gave UNC a 50–47 lead but a three-point play by Ochai Agbaji tied it at 50 with 10:53 left. A three-pointer by Remy Martin gave KU its first lead in more than 19 minutes,

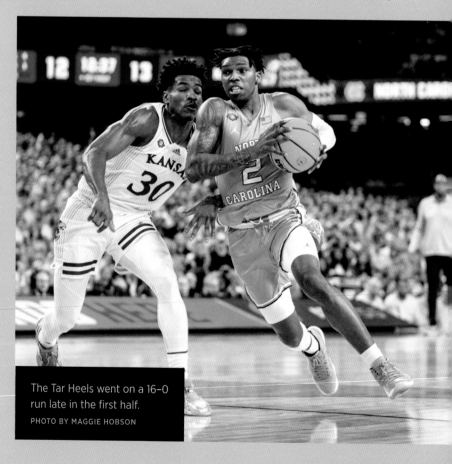

The Tar Heels went on a 16–0 run late in the first half.

PHOTO BY MAGGIE HOBSON

Armando Bacot had a double-double by halftime versus Kansas, which made him the first player with six double-doubles in a single NCAA Tournament.
PHOTO BY MAGGIE HOBSON

and Jalen Wilson tacked on yet another three-point play for a 56–50 lead midway through the half.

Kansas had answered Carolina's 16–0 run late in the first half with its own 31–10 spurt to lead the Tar Heels by six.

Johnson came off the UNC bench for nine second-half points (he finished with 11, just his third double-figure-scoring game of the season), including a three-pointer from the left wing, which knotted the score at 57.

Kansas led for most of the final 10 minutes, with UNC pulling even two times with Johnson's three and again at 65 on a pair of Manek free throws. With 1:41 to play, Manek gave the Tar Heels

their final lead of the season, 69–68, with yet another offensive rebound and tip-in. It would be the only time in the last 10 minutes that Carolina went ahead in a game in which both teams held leads for exactly 18 minutes and 32 seconds.

David McCormack missed a jump hook on the next possession but grabbed the offensive rebound and scored to put KU back in front, 70–69, with 81 seconds to play.

On the ensuing possession, Bacot rolled his right ankle as he drove to the basket. Not only did he lose the ball, but he reinjured his ankle and had to be helped from the floor, his season over with 38 seconds left on the clock.

McCormack scored the game's final points on another jump hook with 22 seconds remaining. Carolina got three shots to even the score, including a three-point attempt by Love as time expired, but to no avail.

Kansas had staged the largest halftime comeback in finals history by shooting 57.6 percent and holding UNC to 27.5 percent from the floor in the second half. The Jayhawks overcame Carolina's 28–8 advantage in second-chance scoring and 55–35 edge on the glass by doubling the Tar Heels in points off turnovers (18–9) and scoring the eventual winning basket on McCormack's putback of his own miss.

After two years of unusual settings and empty arenas, the 2021–22 season also restored the bond between the program and the community. Franklin Street was buzzing on game day again. Undergraduates packed the student section. Tickets were hot commodities.

"The way the fans believe in you at Carolina makes a difference," Manek said. "They kept showing up. At Carolina, we had just lost two games and it was right before Christmas and we were playing Appalachian State, and people are still showing up. You don't realize how abnormal that is. That changes the way you play. We went to Notre Dame and it was one of the most dead basketball games I've ever played in. Then we come back to Chapel Hill and it's packed and you remember, 'Oh, this game is fun.' The fans don't realize the impact they have. That energy they bring in the stands, when you can look up and don't see an empty seat, that makes a difference."

"It felt like we revived the campus and the town of Chapel Hill," Bacot said. "I remember going to Franklin Street that Sunday after the win at Cameron, and it was packed. Everywhere any of the players went, we got recognized everywhere. We had never really experienced this type of love before, we had just heard other players and coaches talk about it. It felt like a turning point in Carolina history."

The community feeling extended beyond the borders of the town of Chapel Hill. Carolina was a popular team in New Orleans, even among those with no vested rooting interest. Representatives from other schools stopped members of the Tar Heels and told them how much they had enjoyed watching Carolina's ride over the last month.

And Hubert Davis couldn't help but notice another group that appreciated the Tar Heels. He was still intent on never making any part of the 2022 Carolina story about him. But he marveled at one consistent message he received: "So many Black men and women working in New Orleans congratulated us and said how much it meant to them to have an African American head coach directing a team in the Final Four," he said.

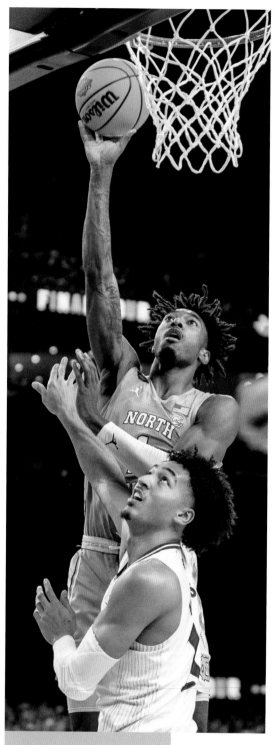

Carolina raced to a 40–25 halftime lead in the national championship game.
PHOTO BY MAGGIE HOBSON

RJ Davis had 11 of his 15 points versus Kansas in the first half.

PHOTO BY MAGGIE HOBSON

Caleb Love made a three, but Carolina was only five for 23 from beyond the arc in the title game.

PHOTO BY MAGGIE HOBSON

Because of the positive experience and the good vibes over the final month of the season, it's easy to lose perspective and believe that the outcome of the 2021–22 season was simple. Just change an offensive strategy here, smile on the sideline there, and that's how you make a national championship contender.

It was never that easy. Hubert Davis cried the night of the national championship loss to Kansas and cried again the next morning when he thought about the events of the past 12 months. It wasn't just the defeat. It was the incredible emotional swings that had accompanied the last 365 days. Being the head coach means something is always happening, and games are often the last refuge from everything else. It means smiling for a photo every time you go into a restaurant. It means everyone needs just "a couple of minutes" with you, from first thing in the morning to last thing at night.

"It's been really hard," Davis said. "And it's been really emotional. You're disappointed because you lost the national championship game. But look at what they accomplished to get there, and that is complete joy. This was probably the hardest year of my life. It's exhausting. I don't know how long it will take to unpack what happened this season."

Not too long ago, Davis was standing at midcourt of the Smith Center talking to his team about the opportunity to hang banners and about the chance to create a legacy. They will put a 2022 Final Four banner in the collection of blue-and-white banners that encircle the Smith Center rafters.

But the most important takeaway from this season might not be found in the rafters.

"The heart of this team was amazing," Bacot said. "We embodied a lot of what Carolina basketball is about. We played hard, smart, and together. We weren't the most talented team in the NCAA Tournament, but we had fight. That's something Coach Davis can hang his hat on. He will use this team as an example for years to come. I can see him telling future teams, 'That 2022 team got blown out four or five times during the regular season, and they made it all the way to the national championship game. If they can do it, you can, too.'

"We weren't even ranked going into the NCAA Tournament, and look how far we made it. Coach Williams had all his stories. Now Coach Davis has a story, too. For as long as he coaches, he's going to tell all his future teams about that 2022 team that came together and that made it further than anyone thought they could." •

ACKNOWLEDGMENTS

We've never done a book like this before.

Steve Kirschner, Matt Bowers, and I have been very fortunate to write three books chronicling Carolina basketball national championships. But those were all books that ended with a win.

We had no idea what the reception might be to a book focusing on a season that ended in a heartbreaking national championship loss to Kansas. Would the players and coaches be willing to talk about it? Would fans want to read it?

We shouldn't have worried. Reliving the 2021–22 season with the Tar Heels was almost as fun as writing about a title, and that's because the people involved made it so enjoyable.

Carolina's Iron Five—Armando Bacot, Leaky Black, RJ Davis, Caleb Love, and Brady Manek—deserve special thanks for sitting down for lengthy interviews in the days immediately following their return from New Orleans and for providing insight they hadn't given before. But all of Carolina's players, including D'Marco Dunn, Duwe Farris, Anthony Harris, Puff Johnson, Rob Landry, Creighton Lebo, Ryan McAdoo, Justin McKoy, Will Shaver, Dontrez Styles, Kerwin Walton, and Jackson Watkins, all helped us better understand the story throughout the course of the season.

You always feel guilty taking a head coach's time for a project like this. Never more so than this year, when the realities of the modern college basketball calendar meant we were asking Hubert Davis for hours of his time for interviews while he was in the middle of trying to determine his 2022–23 roster. But he was consistently gracious and always forthcoming.

The same is true of his staff. Jeff Lebo, Sean May, Brad Frederick, Jackie Manuel, Pat Sullivan, Eric Hoots, Jonas Sahratian, and Doug Halverson were always willing to explain one more game situation or walk through one more scouting report. Shane Parrish is the best BP thrower in the Smith Center and also the best equipment manager. Clint Gwaltney coordinates all the logistics, makes the schedules, and somehow gets everyone to the right place at the right time. The office staff of Cynthia Friend, Kaye Chase, and Bekah Brinkley handled a coaching transition seamlessly. The Tar Heel managers—Kiersten Steinbacher, Virginia Lucas, Drew Goforth, Rob Neill, Shaylen Atma, Will Lam, Alex Pardue, Ragan Copeland, and Riley Whitworth—did endless work for little recognition. Brandon Robinson is clearly the best shooter of any of the managers.

Many of the above people have been involved in books before. We are grateful to Maggie Hobson for her photography and work with the photos in this book for a project we sprung on her roughly about an hour before it was due.

Midway through the NCAA Tournament run, Steve correctly observed that one of the things he'd missed most about a "normal" tournament run was the opportunity to gather for a pregame dinner with so many good people from the traveling party. Thanks to Jones Angell, Bubba Cunningham, John and Sharie Montgomery, and Eric Montross for making those so fun and for keeping a watchful eye on the 11s.

In some form or fashion, every Carolina fan sees the work of a host of others whom they never know by name. Thanks to Ben Alexander, Brett Botta, Ken Cleary, Ray Gaskins, Brandon Gray, John Lanier, John Lawhorne, Robbi Pickeral, Billy Puryear, Josh Reavis, and Ryan Schmitt for always making the Tar Heels look and sound good and travel well.

UNC Press helped us learn about what "supply chain" really means in the year 2022, which essentially means everything needs to be turned in very early. We tried our best to meet the lofty standards set by Mark Simpson-Vos, Dino Battista, Sonya Bonczek, Kim Bryant, Lindsay Starr, Erin Granville, Helen Kyriakoudes, Peter Perez, and John McLeod, all of whom helped make this book what it is.

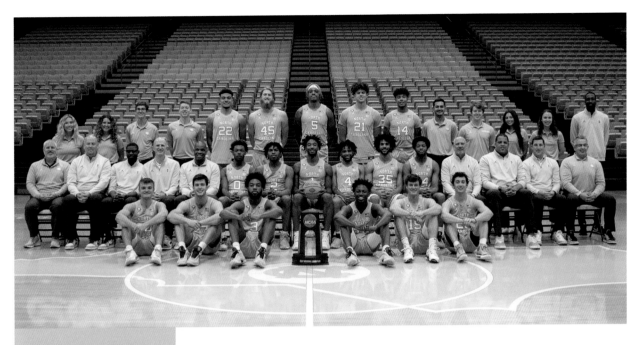

The 2021–22 Tar Heels

Front row (l–r): Jackson Watkins, Duwe Farris, Dontrez Styles, D'Marco Dunn, Rob Landry, Creighton Lebo

Middle row (l–r): Doug Halverson, Pat Sullivan, Jackie Manuel, Brad Frederick, Hubert Davis, Anthony Harris, Caleb Love, Leaky Black, RJ Davis, Ryan McAdoo, Kerwin Walton, Jeff Lebo, Sean May, Eric Hoots, Jonas Sahratian

Back row (l–r): Kiersten Steinbacher, Virginia Lucas, Will Lam, Drew Goforth, Justin McKoy, Brady Manek, Armando Bacot, Will Shaver, Puff Johnson, Shaylen Atma, Rob Neill, Riley Whitworth, Ragan Copeland, Brandon Robinson

PHOTO BY MAGGIE HOBSON

When a basketball season ends, most people naturally assume everyone involved immediately takes some time off. Our families put up with us actually getting busier in the month after the Tar Heels returned from New Orleans. Steve's wife, Jeanne, and kids, Ryan and Emilie, didn't get to New Orleans for this Final Four but put up with his many absences and late nights of game notes and phone calls. Matt loved doing background research for this project by rewatching key games, especially the wins over Duke, with his wife, Crystal, and children Sam and Chloe. Not many jobs provide such pleasant memories. For Adam, having his wife, Jenn, and kids Virginia, Drew, McKay, and Asher together in New Orleans was a season highlight; the chance to spend time together watching Carolina basketball is even more fun than a Mando dunk or an RJ three-pointer. Also, it was another chance for everyone to watch Virginia's highly questionable clapping in person.

A whole new set of Carolina fans fell in love with Tar Heel basketball for the first time this year. It was a thrill to get to experience it through their eyes when they flooded the Smith Center for send-offs and welcome-homes or reacted to stories and videos on GoHeels.com or on social media. Without them, all of us would have to get a real job. We thank you most of all for ensuring that Carolina basketball remains the community experience that makes it so great.

2021-22 SEASON NOTES & STATISTICS

- The Tar Heels went 29-10 with wins in 17 of their last 21 games.
- Carolina advanced to its NCAA-record 21st Final Four and 12th national championship game.
- Kansas defeated the Tar Heels 72-69 in the finals in the New Orleans Superdome.
- It was the third time in the last six NCAA Tournaments the Tar Heels played in the national championship game.
- Carolina defeated four ranked opponents in its last nine games, including at no. 4 Duke, no. 4 Baylor, no. 11 UCLA, and no. 9 Duke in the national semifinals.
- UNC is first all-time in NCAA Tournament wins (131) and Final Fours (21); second in seasons played in the tournament (52), games played (180), tournament winning percentage (.728), and championship game appearances (12); and third in national championships (6).
- Hubert Davis, the winner of the John McLendon Award (CollegeInsider.com) and Big House Gaines Award (National Sports Media Association) as the 2021-22 National Coach of the Year, became the fifth individual to lead his team to the national championship game in his first season as a college head coach.
- It was Carolina's 62nd season with 20 or more wins and its NCAA-record 39th with at least 25.
- The Tar Heels tied Notre Dame for second place in the ACC at 15-5.
- Carolina was the no. 8 seed in the East Region.
- Armando Bacot was the Most Outstanding Player of the East Regional.

- Bacot and Caleb Love both earned All-NCAA Tournament honors in the Final Four and the East Regional; Brady Manek joined them on the all-region team.
- Bacot was the leading vote-getter on the All-ACC first team, and Leaky Black was selected to the league's All-Defensive Team.
- *USA Today* and CBS Sports named Bacot third-team All-America.
- Bacot led Carolina in scoring (16.3), rebounding (13.1), field goal percentage (.569), and blocks (65)—the first player ever to lead the Tar Heels in those four categories in consecutive seasons.
- Bacot led the nation in double-doubles with 31, was second in offensive rebounding (4.2), and third in rebounding.
- Bacot tied David Robinson's (Navy, 1985-86) all-time NCAA single-season record with 31 double-doubles.
- Bacot became the first player in college basketball history with double-doubles in six NCAA Tournament games in a season.
- Bacot shattered the single-season Tar Heel record with 511 rebounds, 95 more than the previous record set by Brice Johnson in 2015-16.
- The 511 rebounds were the fourth most in a season in ACC history; Bacot became the first player with at least 500 since 1956.
- Bacot, Love, and Manek combined to score 1,845 points, the fourth most by three players in UNC history.
- Manek and Love tied for the most points scored by any player in the 2022 Tournament: 113.

- Manek's 22 three-pointers were the most in the tournament and the most ever by a Tar Heel in one NCAA Tournament.
- Manek led UNC this season with 98 threes, second most ever by a Tar Heel.
- Manek shot a career-high 40.3 percent from three-point range, which led the ACC.
- Manek scored 28 points against Marquette and 26 against Baylor. He became the fifth Tar Heel to score at least 26 points in consecutive NCAA games.
- RJ Davis and Love became the first Tar Heels to score 30 points in consecutive NCAA Tournament games—Davis had 30 against Baylor and Love scored 30 versus UCLA.
- Davis's 12 assists versus Marquette equaled the second most by a Tar Heel in NCAA play.
- Black became one of four Tar Heels to amass 600 career points, 500 rebounds, 250 assists, 100 steals, and 50 blocks with George Lynch, David Noel, and Danny Green.
- The Tar Heels led the ACC in free throw shooting at 76.4 percent, their second-best percentage ever.
- Love made 40 consecutive free throws, the second-longest streak in UNC history.
- Carolina made a school-record 328 three-pointers this season, breaking the previous high of 312 in 2018-19.
- The Tar Heels led the ACC and were third in the country in rebound margin at plus-8.2 per game.

2021-22 North Carolina Men's Basketball
39-Game Stats

Game Records

Record	Overall	Home	Away	Neutral
ALL GAMES	29-10	15-2	8-3	6-5
CONFERENCE	15-5	8-2	7-3	0-0
NON-CONFERENCE	14-5	7-0	1-0	6-5

Score by Periods

Team	1st	2nd	OT	TOT
North Carolina	1446	1548	44	3038
Opponents	1266	1493	21	2780

Team Box Score

No.	Player	GP-GS	MIN	AVG	FG-FGA	FG%	3FG-3FGA	3FG%	FT-FTA	FT%	OFF	DEF	TOT	AVG	PF	DQ	A	TO	BLK	STL	PTS	AVG
5	BACOT, Armando	39-39	1236:34	31.7	244-429	.569	1-8	.125	146-218	.670	163	348	511	13.1	112	5	59	77	65	33	635	16.3
2	LOVE, Caleb	39-38	1331:11	34.1	198-534	.371	93-258	.360	132-153	.863	8	125	133	3.4	68	1	139	106	9	37	621	15.9
45	MANEK, Brady	39-27	1186:50	30.4	219-444	.493	98-243	.403	53-76	.697	58	179	237	6.1	65	1	70	59	27	23	589	15.1
4	DAVIS, RJ	39-39	1320:54	33.9	178-419	.425	66-180	.367	105-126	.833	22	144	166	4.3	84	0	142	74	8	40	527	13.5
13	GARCIA, Dawson	16-12	328:33	20.5	47-116	.405	12-32	.375	38-48	.792	33	55	88	5.5	34	1	11	21	5	7	144	9.0
1	BLACK, Leaky	38-38	1127:04	29.7	68-146	.466	17-51	.333	33-38	.868	49	113	162	4.3	63	0	104	37	26	34	186	4.9
24	WALTON, Kerwin	31-1	414:21	13.4	38-102	.373	23-65	.354	7-7	1.000	7	31	38	1.2	33	0	13	18	4	7	106	3.4
14	JOHNSON, Puff	24-0	250:40	10.4	28-61	.459	6-26	.231	13-18	.722	18	29	47	2.0	26	0	11	3	4	7	75	3.1
0	HARRIS, Anthony	14-0	166:39	11.9	13-27	.481	3-5	.600	8-9	.889	2	3	5	0.4	17	0	9	11	0	2	37	2.6
3	STYLES, Dontrez	30-0	173:60	5.8	24-55	.436	3-18	.167	8-15	.533	11	32	43	1.4	16	0	2	11	2	5	59	2.0
22	MCKOY, Justin	30-0	208:19	6.9	8-36	.222	3-12	.250	12-15	.800	12	30	42	1.4	31	0	14	13	3	3	31	1.0
11	DUNN, D'Marco	23-0	94:19	4.1	9-31	.290	3-15	.200	1-3	.333	1	6	7	0.3	8	0	7	6	0	1	22	1.0
34	FARRIS, Duwe	6-0	09:17	1.5	2-2	1.000	0-0	.000	1-2	.500	1	2	3	0.5	3	0	0	0	0	0	5	0.8
30	WATKINS, Jackson	3-0	03:01	1.0	0-2	.000	0-1	.000	1-2	.500	0	2	2	0.7	2	0	1	0	0	1	1	0.3
25	LEBO, Creighton	5-0	07:28	1.5	0-2	.000	0-1	.000	0-0	.000	0	0	0	0.0	0	0	0	2	0	1	0	0.0
35	MCADOO, Ryan	7-1	12:49	1.8	0-3	.000	0-1	.000	0-0	.000	1	2	3	0.4	2	0	0	1	0	1	0	0.0
15	LANDRY, Rob	3-0	03:01	1.0	0-0	.000	0-0	.000	0-0	.000	0	0	0	0.0	0	0	0	1	0	0	0	0.0
	Team										61	60	121					15				
	Total	39	7875		1076-2409	.447	328-916	.358	558-730	.764	447	1161	1608	41.2	564	8	582	455	153	202	3038	77.9
	Opponents	39	7875		1048-2464	.425	301-893	.337	383-528	.725	319	956	1275	32.7	645	12	498	378	139	259	2780	71.3

Team Statistics

	UNC	OPP
Scoring	3038	2780
Points per game	77.9	71.3
Scoring margin	+6.6	-
Field goals-att	1076-2409	1048-2464
Field goal pct	.447	.425
3 point fg-att	328-916	301-893
3-point FG pct	.358	.337
3-pt FG made per game	8.4	7.7
Free throws-att	558-730	383-528
Free throw pct	.764	.725
F-Throws made per game	14.3	9.8
Rebounds	1608	1275
Rebounds per game	41.2	32.7
Rebounding margin	+8.5	-
Assists	582	498
Assists per game	14.9	12.8
Turnovers	455	378
Turnovers per game	11.7	9.7
Turnover margin	-2.0	-
Assist/turnover ratio	1.3	1.3
Steals	202	259
Steals per game	5.2	6.6
Blocks	153	139
Blocks per game	3.9	3.6
Winning streak	0	-
Home win streak	2	-
Attendance	315115	97771
Home games-Avg/Game	17-18536	11-8888
Neutral site-Avg/Game	-	11-23249

Team Results

Date	Opponent		Score	Att.
11/09/2021	Loyola Maryland	W	83-67	14992
11/12/2021	Brown	W	94-87	16854
11/16/2021	at Col. of Charleston	W	94-83	5203
11/20/2021	vs Purdue	L	84-93	9176
11/21/2021	vs Tennessee	L	72-89	9100
11/23/2021	UNC Asheville	W	72-53	15710
12/01/2021	Michigan	W	72-51	19938
12/05/2021	at Georgia Tech	W	79-62	6217
12/11/2021	Elon	W	80-63	16607
12/14/2021	Furman	W	74-61	14342
12/18/2021	vs Kentucky	L	69-98	12117
12/21/2021	Appalachian St.	W	70-50	19386
01/02/2022	at Boston College	W	91-65	5516
01/05/2022	at Notre Dame	L	73-78	6259
01/08/2022	Virginia	W	74-58	20638
01/15/2022	Georgia Tech	W	88-65	18568
01/18/2022	at Miami (FL)	L	57-85	5979
01/22/2022	at Wake Forest	L	76-98	11898
01/24/2022	Virginia Tech	W	78-68	19357
01/26/2022	Boston College	W	58-47	17237
01/29/2022	NC State	W	100-80	21750
02/01/2022	at Louisville	Wot	90-83	13386
02/05/2022	Duke	L	67-87	21750
02/08/2022	at Clemson	W	79-77	7470
02/12/2022	Florida St.	W	94-74	20348
02/16/2022	Pittsburgh	L	67-76	17270
02/19/2022	at Virginia Tech	W	65-57	9825
02/21/2022	Louisville	W	70-63	18618
02/26/2022	at NC State	W	84-74	16704
02/28/2022	Syracuse	Wot	88-79	21750
03/05/2022	at Duke	W	94-81	9314
03/10/2022	vs Virginia	W	63-43	15994
03/11/2022	vs Virginia Tech	L	59-72	15994
03/17/2022	vs Marquette	W	95-63	12964
03/19/2022	vs Baylor	Wot	93-86	0
03/25/2022	vs UCLA	W	73-66	20136
03/27/2022	vs Saint Peter's	W	69-49	20235
04/02/2022	vs Duke	W	81-77	70602
04/04/2022	vs Kansas	L	69-72	69423

2021-22 North Carolina Men's Basketball
NCAA Tournament Games

Game Records

Record	Overall	Home	Away	Neutral
ALL GAMES	5-1	0-0	0-0	5-1
CONFERENCE	0-0	0-0	0-0	0-0
NON-CONFERENCE	5-1	0-0	0-0	5-1

Score by Periods

Team	1st	2nd	OT	TOT
North Carolina	235	232	13	480
Opponents	166	241	6	413

Team Box Score

No.	Player	GP-GS	MIN	AVG	FG-FGA	FG%	3FG-3FGA	3FG%	FT-FTA	FT%	OFF	DEF	TOT	AVG	PF	DQ	A	TO	BLK	STL	PTS	AVG
2	LOVE, Caleb	6-6	220:49	36.8	40-106	.377	19-58	.328	14-18	.778	2	18	20	3.3	14	1	14	19	2	1	113	18.8
45	MANEK, Brady	6-6	211:30	35.2	38-70	.543	22-46	.478	15-21	.714	13	36	49	8.2	13	0	8	8	9	1	113	18.8
5	BACOT, Armando	6-6	204:10	34.0	30-71	.423	0-0	.000	32-54	.593	38	61	99	16.5	18	1	12	12	9	4	92	15.3
4	DAVIS, RJ	6-6	226:28	37.7	25-79	.316	9-32	.281	29-31	.935	8	31	39	6.5	14	0	30	12	0	5	88	14.7
14	JOHNSON, Puff	6-0	67:40	11.3	13-21	.619	2-6	.333	2-3	.667	3	11	14	2.3	7	0	2	0	1	1	30	5.0
1	BLACK, Leaky	6-6	215:51	36.0	10-25	.400	2-9	.222	3-4	.750	11	16	27	4.5	13	0	23	7	5	7	25	4.2
3	STYLES, Dontrez	5-0	48:44	9.7	7-14	.500	1-6	.167	0-0	.000	1	11	12	2.4	6	0	2	4	0	2	15	3.0
24	WALTON, Kerwin	2-0	04:59	2.5	1-2	.500	0-1	.000	0-0	.000	2	0	2	1.0	1	0	0	0	0	0	2	1.0
22	MCKOY, Justin	5-0	17:39	3.5	0-4	.000	0-2	.000	2-2	1.000	1	3	4	0.8	3	0	1	3	0	1	2	0.4
34	FARRIS, Duwe	1-0	00:45	0.7	0-0	.000	0-0	.000	0-0	.000	0	0	0	0.0	0	0	0	0	0	0	0	0.0
25	LEBO, Creighton	1-0	00:45	0.7	0-1	.000	0-1	.000	0-0	.000	0	0	0	0.0	0	0	0	0	0	1	0	0.0
35	MCADOO, Ryan	1-0	00:45	0.7	0-1	.000	0-1	.000	0-0	.000	0	1	1	1.0	0	0	0	0	0	0	0	0.0
11	DUNN, D'Marco	2-0	04:59	2.5	0-1	.000	0-0	.000	0-0	.000	0	1	1	0.5	1	0	1	0	0	0	0	0.0
	Team										16	12	28					5				
	Total	6	1225		164-395	.415	55-162	.340	97-133	.729	95	201	296	49.3	90	2	93	70	26	23	480	80.0
	Opponents	6	1225		159-414	.384	37-137	.270	58-87	.667	67	151	218	36.3	105	3	71	47	32	39	413	68.8

Team Statistics

	UNC	OPP
Scoring	**480**	**413**
Points per game	80.0	68.8
Scoring margin	+11.2	-
Field goals-att	**164-395**	**159-414**
Field goal pct	.415	.384
3 point fg-att	**55-162**	**37-137**
3-point FG pct	.340	.270
3-pt FG made per game	9.2	6.2
Free throws-att	**97-133**	**58-87**
Free throw pct	.729	.667
F-Throws made per game	16.2	9.7
Rebounds	**296**	**218**
Rebounds per game	49.3	36.3
Rebounding margin	+13.0	-
Assists	**93**	**71**
Assists per game	15.5	11.8
Turnovers	**70**	**47**
Turnovers per game	11.7	7.8
Turnover margin	-3.8	-
Assist/turnover ratio	1.3	1.5
Steals	**23**	**39**
Steals per game	3.8	6.5
Blocks	**26**	**32**
Blocks per game	4.3	5.3
Winning streak	**0**	**-**
Home win streak	0	-
Attendance	**0**	**0**
Home games-Avg/Game	0-0	0-0
Neutral site-Avg/Game	-	6-32227

Team Results

Date	Opponent		Score	Att.
03/17/2022	vs Marquette	W	95-63	12964
03/19/2022	vs Baylor	Wot	93-86	0
03/25/2022	vs UCLA	W	73-66	20136
03/27/2022	vs Saint Peter's	W	69-49	20235
04/02/2022	vs Duke	W	81-77	70602
04/04/2022	vs Kansas	L	69-72	69423